SEASHORE
IDENTIFIER

SEASHORE
IDENTIFIER

BOB LOLLO

MALLARD
PRESS

A QUINTET BOOK

An imprint of BDD Promotional
Book Company Inc.
666 Fifth Avenue, New York, NY 10103

Mallard Press and its accompanying design and
logo are trademarks of
BDD Promotional Book Company, Inc.

First published in the United States of America
in 1992 by the Mallard Press

ISBN 0-7924-5519-3

This book was designed and produced by
Quintet Publishing Limited
6 Blundell Street
London N7 9BH

Creative Director: Terry Jeavons
Designer: Annie Moss
Project Editors: Caroline Beattie, Lindsay Porter
Editor: Sean Callery
Picture Researcher: Bob Lollo
Illustrators: Vana Hegarty and
Danny McBride

Typeset in Great Britain by
Central Southern Typesetters, Eastbourne
Manufactured in Singapore by Eray Scan (Pte) Ltd
Printed in Singapore by Star Standard Industries Pte Ltd

CONTENTS

INTRODUCTION: THE SEA

his book is all about what you might find when you visit the seashore. One thing you are guaranteed to see but which it is easy to ignore as you search for interesting animals and plants on the shore is perhaps the most mysterious part of our planet: the sea.

The sea occupies about 70 per cent of the Earth's surface – taking up 1,300 million cubic kilometres of space. Underneath the waves the sea bed is not flat and regular: it is as varied a landscape as we find on all the land we occupy. The sea-bed is a vast area with mountains, valleys and plateaux. Its deepest point is the base of a canyon in Mariana Trench, east of the Mariana Islands in the north-west Pacific Ocean. Here the

OPPOSITE *Waves break against a rock ledge just offshore, throwing water high into the air.*

BELOW *The sea's debris is washed up on the shore, evidence of the many forms of life it sustains within its waters.*

distance to the sea surface is 36,201 ft (11,034 m) – far deeper than the height of our tallest mountain, Mount Everest. Light hardly penetrates the depths of the sea, so there are many creatures which live in complete darkness, using senses other than sight to know where they are. At these deep levels, the effects of the changing seasons are much delayed: while it is winter up above, the warmth from the summer sun is just reaching the dark waters.

The sea is a magical thing, for its waters contain every mineral known to man – including gold, and 13 million tons of silver – all held in a solution. One element accounts for three quarters of the materials held diluted in seawater: sodium chloride, better known as salt. Water also holds a lot of oxygen, which is essential to all life forms. When oxygen is breathed, carbon dioxide is expelled – and this in turn is vital in the life cycle of plants.

The seas of the world are the home of countless life forms, from the smallest (bacteria) to the largest (the whale). If you fill up a bucket with seawater, it will contain thousands of living things – most of them invisible to the naked eye. At the bottom of the scale is plankton, which is the word for many tiny forms of life which float in and on the sea, providing food for many plants and creatures. Plankton sustains even the largest animals – a blue whale, for example, grows from 15 to 75 tonnes in two years, purely from eating plankton.

All life in the sea is inter-dependent, which means that each creature and plant has a function which helps keep the sea alive. So animals which eat the plants on the sea-bed form a food supply for carnivores, or meat eaters, in the sea above them, who in turn are preyed on by more carnivores (such as the shark). When any of these creatures defecates or dies, it releases nutrients which fall to the sea-bed and help new plants to grow. It is a complex process which the activities of man, through pollution and over-fishing, tend to threaten.

So next time you are at the seashore, take a look at the sea, and remember its size and importance to our planet.

THE SANDY BEACHES

LEFT *Many beaches are covered with the sea's debris, whether shells or stones. These objects, thrown onto the shore by the waves, provide endless opportunities for 'beach-combing'. Examine a shell . . . which creature lived there? What minerals make up the various pebbles in the sand?*

Where land meets sea lies an undefined area which constantly shifts back and forth, an ever-changing boundary where the waves, tides and winds work tirelessly to reclaim what the sea believes it owns. The land reacts more quietly, building its defences against the next storm, reclaiming its losses a little at a time. What is beach this year may be a sand bar some distance from the beach in years to come. By the end of the following year, the sand from that sand bar could reside on top of a dune, well away from the sea.

However, there is more to the seashore than change alone. There are wading birds with long legs extended behind them, flying over hidden coves, sea ducks bobbing on the waves in a quiet bay, and gulls searching the beach for food at changing tides.

The ebb and flood tides affect life on the beach where small animals live in the wet sands of the

MAKING A MARINE AQUARIUM

THINGS TO DO

You could make your own seaside by adapting an aquarium to make it into a marine aquarium. Then you can collect some creatures and plants from the shore and keep them alive in your own home. The aquarium must be kept out of direct sunlight.

The diagram shows what you will need – don't forget the pebbles, plastic sheet and sand at the base, or the sheet of glass or plastic for the top to stop the water evaporating.

When you collect the sea water pour it gently down the side of the glass so that you do not disturb the bottom too much. If it needs to be topped up, you could use a little tap water but sea water is preferable.

At the beach, collect your specimens in plastic containers with tight lids and keep them in a cool box. Do not take too much: some seaweed, a couple of rock creatures and some sand lovers will be plenty. Make sure you do not put in too many predators such as crabs as they will eat all your specimens, and remember to put food such as small pieces of fish and mussels in regularly.

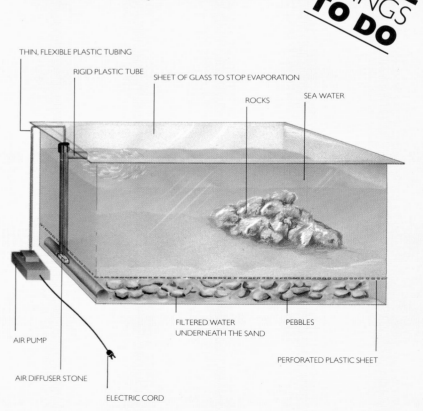

THIN, FLEXIBLE PLASTIC TUBING

RIGID PLASTIC TUBE

SHEET OF GLASS TO STOP EVAPORATION

ROCKS

SEA WATER

FILTERED WATER UNDERNEATH THE SAND

PEBBLES

PERFORATED PLASTIC SHEET

AIR PUMP

AIR DIFFUSER STONE

ELECTRIC CORD

intertidal zones, and sea wrack (or rockweed) lies in windrows at the high tide mark. Jetsam and flotsam are pushed onto the beach by the gentle wave action, cleansing the sea of debris from passing ships, and washed up dead sea animals are a reminder of the harsh life beneath the waves.

The lives of the flora and fauna at the seashore depend on the tidal actions and their effect on the growth of the plants and animals that live on the edge of the sea. The tides bring them the oxygen and nourishment that they need to grow and live. Certain small animals and plants living in the intertidal zones spend part of their lives outside water but are still dependent upon it for survival.

Going to the beach

In the early 1800s, the beach was generally considered a place for rehabilitation of the sick rather than somewhere for relaxation by Europeans and North Americans. The sea was thought to provide a cure for deafness, ulcers, asthma and consumption, and so began the hotels and the health resorts along the coasts. Early bathers remained

ABOVE Sand from the shore area to the left has been transported by longshore currents, which deposited the sand offshore. The bar is covered by water at high tide but the waves breaking off shore reveal its presence. The deeper blue water indicates the edge of the bar.

ENJOYING THE BEACH

You may need the following equipment: net, binoculars, notebook and pencil, bucket, plastic containers and a spade. However, you can have a lot of fun without these things. Remember to put back any creatures you pick up to examine where you found them, making sure that they are protected from the sun if you moved a rock. Never eat anything you find on the beach.

fully clothed, and ladies and gentlemen never bathed together, each having their own dipper (used for dipping reluctant persons in the cold seas) and their own section of the beach.

As the beach holiday became more popular, with elaborate picnics and children and nurses armed with pails and shovels, an invention was sought to get away from the disadvantages of beach holidays: wet sand and salt water, which was damaging to leather and cloth. The complaints gave birth to the American boardwalk, and once the boardwalk was erected, businesses began to spring up along the walk offering all sorts of pleasures to the passerby.

But children of all ages continue to play in the sand, digging and building, drawing sand pictures, destroying and building anew: castles are the most popular, with drawings of fish and birds following closely behind. And the beach is the beginning and ending point for surfers, who put out to sea just beyond the breakers hoping for the just-right wave to deposit both them and their surfboards back on the beach, although not until they have cut and turned and twisted, using the entire force of the wave to display their skills.

Who lives on the beach?

However, there is more to the sandy beaches than our enjoyment. They have always been an important part of the life cycle of other animals that also use the sand. Various sea birds worldwide use portions of the beach area to build their nests and raise their young. Gulls and terns are common, and several birds which are now endangered build nests on the beach. Where possible, nesting areas are roped off to prevent any disturbance by beach users.

The shore also provides a resting place for migrating birds. They can depend upon the edge of the sea to provide them with food to replenish their bodies from the strenuous flight just passed and the long flight ahead. Migrations tend to coincide with the availability of food in the form of eggs being laid on the beach or small fish close to the shore or in salt marshes.

The grunion fish lives on the west coast of America and lays its eggs on the beach. Grunion hunting on some California beaches is popular, but can be very frustrating. The grunion lays its eggs at night just after the highest point of the spring tide. The male and female come ashore on the tide, then work their way to the top of the tide. The female buries herself tail first in the sand with only her head exposed. She deposits her eggs in the moist stand while the male curls around her depositing his sperm, and they then

ABOVE *This ruddy turnstone has travelled south and is in its winter plumage.*

BELOW *The phases of the moon play an important part in the spawning period of the grunion. This small, silver-coloured fish deposits its eggs on the sand at night after high tide. Tides are highest when the moon is new or full.*

wiggle back to the water. If the eggs are not washed out by a succeeding tide or dried out by the sun, or eaten by hungry birds, the high water of the next spring tide will engulf them. A membrane surrounding the baby fish will dissolve and the fry will swim down the forebeach to the sea. If this spring tide does not reach the eggs and surround them, the tiny fish will lie dormant until the next one.

Waves carrying eggs and young to distant shores ensure that life continues in the ocean. They bring new life to the island shores and continental shores where a particular life form may not have previously existed. As long as there are predictable ocean currents, there will be new life growing along the shores and in the salt flats.

The part of the beach that slopes into the water is called the foreshore. The offshore beach is the submerged portion that cannot be seen or that portion of the beach lying underwater next to the foreshore. The area just above the high tide mark is called the berm, and the berm becomes the corridor between high tide and the foredunes. An inspection of the grains of sand on the upper beach reveals that these have a frosted appearance due to being tossed about by the winds. When sand grains strike each other, the grains develop rough edges and the frosted appearance results from the force of impact.

The dry berm is vastly different from the moist intertidal zone, and the difference in environments means a difference in life existing in the two areas. The animal life on the upper beach is much advanced from the life in the wet sand, although it is still fairly primitive. The most advanced animal is the ghost crab which spends its life on the dry sand but must moisten its gills by returning periodically to the sea. Because of its evolution of moving from the sea to land, its legs are no longer designed for swimming and the crab does not enter the water to swim, although its offspring begin their lives in sea water.

Beach fleas are one of the successful animals that have nearly severed their ties with the ocean. They burrow in the dry sand above high tide and come out at night to feed on the bits of both plant and animal that have washed ashore in the intertidal zone of wet sand during the high tide.

The remaining life on the berm is confined to beetle life among the sea wrack, a few centipedes, millipedes and flies. Beach hoppers and pillbugs are in among other tiny animals looking for a meal in the wrack, the sole food supply available.

As you wander along the beach peering down for signs of life in the sand, don't forget to look up and listen, too – for you will find many kinds of bird here as well. Birds find much to feed on near the seashore: some hunt for fish in the shallow waters; others prey on the many creatures in

RIGHT *Knotted sea wrack is home and food to life on the upper part of the beach, the berm. The beetles, centipedes and flies that live among the wrack will in turn attract birds looking for food.*

BELOW *A brown pelican dives for food among the waves.*

the sand such as starfish, crabs and cockles. With their beady eyes, quick reflexes and perfectly formed wings, birds are well equipped to survive in the seashore habitat. Most of the birds live near the seashore for the breeding season, and spend the rest of their time on the open sea.

If you are able to visit the beach every day it is well worth keeping an eye on one area where birds are active as you will have the pleasure of identifying nesting sites, spotting regulars and intruders – perhaps even finding out what some of them prefer to eat! However at home they look, remember that many of these birds migrate long distances to follow the seasons around the earth. They are able to fly thousands of miles across the sea and still find last year's nesting ground.

Bird life

'Seagulls' is the popular term for the gull family which includes a number of birds, and with practice you will soon learn to tell them apart. There are common gulls, herring gulls, lesser and greater black-backs, and black-headed gulls, for example. On a sandy beach you are most likely to spot a herring gull. This is a strong and aggressive bird which sometimes picks up cockles from the sand and flies above a hard surface such as rocks or even the promenade, dropping its victim to the ground to break open the shell. It has a broad bill useful for attacking all kinds of prey.

The oystercatcher is another frequent predator on sandy beaches, picking at cockles with its long, powerful red beak, with which it can often force open the hapless mollusc's protective shell.

Oystercatchers can often be seen stalking along the beach in groups, excitedly crying out when food is spotted.

The little tern is the smallest of the tern family, and like its relations is a great traveller. It prefers the habitat of a sandy or gravelly seashore. It breeds in Europe, Asia, Africa, North America and Australia, and spends the winter anywhere between the Mediterranean and South Africa.

ABOVE *Ruddy turnstones search among the debris for their next meal.*

BELOW *The oystercatcher can be recognized by its long red beak, which enables it to force open the shells of the molluscs on which it feeds.*

The turnstone is a clever, small bird with a short bill that curves slightly upwards. It uses this to turn over stones, seashells and seaweed in its search for food – hence its name. It breeds in the coastal tundra of Eurasia, North America and Scandinavia, migrating for the winter in Australia, Africa and South America.

Crabs and shrimps

One of the most common sights on sandy beaches shortly after the tide has gone out is one of the crab family resting in a puddle. Crabs are crustaceans, a class of arthropod which also includes creatures such as lobsters, shrimps, barnacles and woodlice. Arthropods are invertebrates (animals with no backbone) with jointed legs and a segmented body.

Crabs have ten legs, although they only use four pairs for walking – others act as pairs of pincers to grab food and fend off attackers. One of the remarkable things about crabs is that they can snap off one of these legs voluntarily through

a muscle contraction – very handy if a predator is holding on to it! The limb eventually grows back.

Crabs scurry sideways with a distinctive movement – their legs are jointed so that this is the only way they can move. They are great scavengers, eating anything they can find, and usually hunt for food at night when submerged by the tide. The rest of the time they hide in crevices and under boulders. Crabs have sharp pincers which can give you a nasty nip if you try to pick them up. Much less dangerous are their old shells: crabs moult every so often, swelling up their bodies with water to break their shell, revealing a new, soft shell which grows and takes two weeks to harden, during which time the crab stays in hiding as much as possible.

Therefore, crab shells found lying on the beach may not indicate a crab has died, but that the shell has been discarded for a new and larger one. The masked crab has long pincers and short legs which it uses to dig itself down in the sand leaving only the tips in its antennae above the surface. These form a tube which takes in sea water and filters out sand, leaving oxygen for breathing. You may find a dead masked crab on the shore: they have markings like a human face on their shells, and are straw-coloured.

ABOVE *The black-headed gull can be recognized instantly by its bold markings. Gulls are aggressive predators, and will circle above the shores and waves before swooping down to strike their prey.*

RIGHT *This female rock crab carries her orange eggmass on the underside of her body to protect the eggs from predators.*

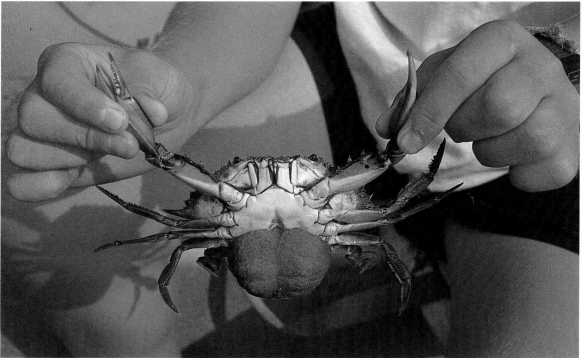

ABOVE *This pretty crab, the calico, is found in Florida. It is a treat to find a calico crab's shell on the beach because it is so colourful. If you find an empty shell, it is because the crab has shed it to grow another, larger, one.*

LEFT *The safest way to hold a crab without being pinched! This view of the crab clearly shows the segmented body common to all arthropods.*

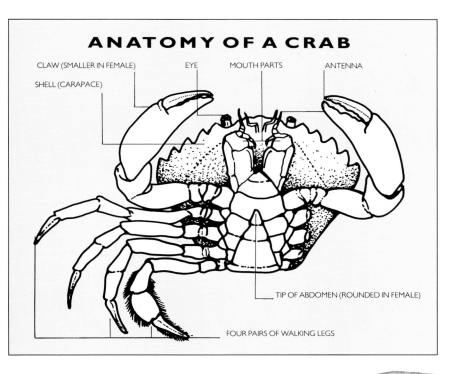

ANATOMY OF A CRAB

CLAW (SMALLER IN FEMALE)   EYE   MOUTH PARTS   ANTENNA

SHELL (CARAPACE)

TIP OF ABDOMEN (ROUNDED IN FEMALE)

FOUR PAIRS OF WALKING LEGS

live on sandy shores (mostly bivalves) and others prefer to inhabit rocks (mostly gastropods) – there are examples of rock-living molluscs in the following chapter, *The Rocky Coasts*.

Bivalve shells have two parts, hinged together by a piece of ligament. Typical examples are mussels, razorshells, clams and oysters. Most that you find you will be open as the mollusc has left the shell, or perhaps been pecked out by a predatory bird. If you find one that is still occupied and you disturb the mollusc, it will clamp the shell halves together so tight that you will not be able to open them.

Gastropod shells are more rounded and when you look inside they seem to be built around a column in a spiral shape. This is because the shell has grown as a coiled tube around the body of the mollusc. Typical examples are whelks,

The edible crab can be found on the beach but will live as far as 325ft (100m) under the sea. A tropical crab which travels the other way is the robber crab, which has been known to scuttle up palm trees and eat the coconuts.

Shrimps and prawns are two often-confused inhabitants of the sandy beach. The shrimp is there for much of the year, buried just below the sea surface in shallow water, watching out for prey with its little antennae. Prawns look much the same (except they have fatter bodies) but generally inhabit warmer deeper water, moving into the seashore shallows in the summer. Going shrimping is one of the joys of the beach. You need a shrimping net (which forms a half circle with a straight bar at its base). This is pushed gently through shallow water, pushing just below the surface of the sand. Pollution and increased presence of humans limits catches today, but you can still have a lot of fun and imagine your ancestors doing this to catch their next meal.

ABOVE *The boat shell or slipper shell has a curiously modified shell, having a half deck on the lower surface. Each of these shells in its lifetime is first male, then female. In chains of attached shells, those at the bottom are always females.*

Shells

Shells are easy to find on the beach and some are beautifully and delicately coloured. Each shell you come across has its own story, for shells are the old homes of molluscs. There are more than 120,000 types of mollusc in the world, and most have a soft body (which is why they live in protective shells) and one foot. There are two main kinds of mollusc: bivalves and gastropods. Some

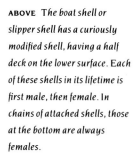

RIGHT *Shells on the beach reveal the harsh life of sea creatures along the shores and under the seas. Shore birds, fond of the morsels living within the bivalves, add to the yearly mortality. These shells will be ground by the waves into particles of sand.*

winkles and conch shells. Gastropod means 'stomach foot', because these molluscs seem to slide on their stomachs like a snail.

If you look carefully at these shells, you will find concentric rings and lines. These indicate patterns of growth: when there is plenty of food for the mollusc, the shell grows quickly; when there is less to eat, it uses up its energy just surviving.

Some bivalve molluscs burrow deep into the sand to find food and safety. Tellins and razorshells can often be found on sandy beaches after a storm has churned the sand around. Sometimes they are on the surface, but all can burrow into the sand – some as far as 16 yards (15 metres). They are said to be able to burrow down faster than a human can dig. They do this by extending their foot down and using it as an anchor to pull the rest of their body behind.

Razorshells are so-called because they resemble old-fashioned cut-throat razors with their two long, thin halves. They are very fast burrowers but often leave an impression in the sand rather like a key-

ABOVE A selection of lighting whelk shells. The whelk is a spiral mollusc which travels about by using its large, flat, muscular foot. Nearly all these gastropods are 'right handed', with the opening to the right as it faces the observer. These are univalves, or in one piece, as opposed to clams, which are bivalves.

RIGHT The jingle shell's upper valve is perforated by a hole for the passage of a strong byssus cord that attaches the jingle to a rock or other shell. The shell comes in colours of silver, gold and apricot and is found in windrows, being gently shifted by the tides.

hole. If you tip a little salt down one of these impressions, the angry razorshell will soon appear to find out what is going on.

The common cockle is up to 2in (5cm) across and has 24–28 ribs which form the familiar shell shape. It lives in sand, gravel or mud on the lower shore and shallow water.

The common whelk has a high, thick shell up to 4in (10cm) long.

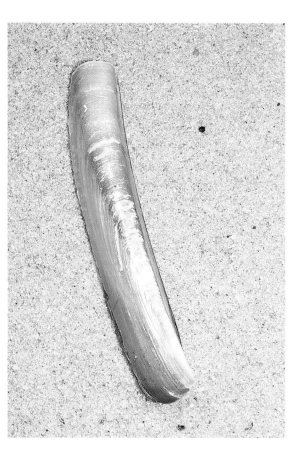

LEFT *The razor clam has a long muscular foot for digging which permits the clam to move through the sand faster than a person can dig with their hands. It lies vertically in the sand with the foot stretched below it in anticipation of a quick retreat beneath the sandy beach.*

Life in the sand

Walk towards the sea on a sandy beach when the tide is out, and you will very likely find yourself approaching anglers who send their baited hooks flying out into the sea. But they don't spend all their time looking for signs of a bite. They work with spades too. They are digging for worms in the wet sand: worms that will offer juicy temptation to the fish of the sea. But how do these worms survive in their airless homes? How do the anglers know where to dig?

The lugworm is easily located by the worm casts it leaves on the sand. These look a bit like pieces of spaghetti coated in mud, and once you have seen them you will find them everywhere you go. Worm casts are waste matter from the lugworm's home. This creature lives under the sand in a U-shaped tunnel lined with mucus. The worm eats the sand washed in at one entrance, digests the minerals, and deposits the remains out of the tunnel exit. It can grow up to 8in (20cm) long. Lugworms stay in their cosy burrows for weeks at a time, but are targets for birds and fish (when the tide is in) as well as those digging fishermen.

The lugworm is just one of many kinds of worm which live in the sand and wait for food to come to them rather than hunt it down. Such worms carry out the same function as earthworms on land, of cleansing and powdering the sand as they eat.

Some distant relations of the lugworm are absolutely massive. In 1979 huge sea worms 10ft (3m) long were found 8,000ft (2,450m) deep under the Pacific Ocean near the Galapagos Islands. Like the lugworm, they were living in tubes created by their own excretions.

THE LUGWORM'S BURROW

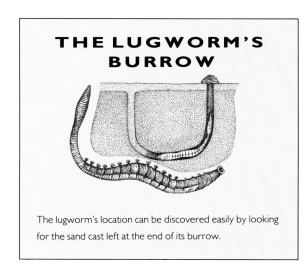

The lugworm's location can be discovered easily by looking for the sand cast left at the end of its burrow.

THE SEA TURTLE'S NEST

Like the lugworm, the sea turtle depends on the sandy beach for its existence – but for very different reasons. The sandy beach is an essential place in the life of a sea turtle. The large adult female lumbers onto the dry sand above high tide to lay her eggs in a shallow hole she digs with her front flippers. She lays her eggs, up to 125 per nest, then covers the leathery eggs with sand. The burning sunshine provides the heat that is needed to develop the tiny turtles. The mother leaves the nest as soon as the eggs are covered, and she is rested enough to make the return journey back to the sea. When the young are hatched, they must fend for themselves and have an instinct to turn to the ocean after they work their way through the loose sand. In many parts of the world, sea birds seem to know instinctively when the eggs hatch. They circle the beaches, watching for the baby turtles to run down to the water from their nest on the upper beach. Once located, these birds dive down swooping close to the sand, picking up baby turtles in their beaks.

Those turtles who reach the water are still subject to attack from sea creatures. So much so that only two or three turtles out of the 125 will live to become adults. Many nests do not hatch any eggs because raccoons and foxes have a fondness for turtle eggs. They dig them up soon after the female lays her eggs.

People have a general disregard for the safety of the eggs and eating steaks from an adult sea turtle is popular. Worldwide, concerned people are banding together to save the turtle from extinction by preserving egg-laying on beaches as tourism and development threaten their future. These patrols

The green seaturtle is one of the species of sea turtles that has been protected. This one was probably born on an American beach.

have people on watch around the clock, ready to gather the baby turtles before anything can happen to them. In some cases, the eggs are taken from the nests and hatched in incubators, releasing the tiny turtles directly into the sea, and some beaches are roped off at egg-laying time to protect the females and their young.

Starfish and jellyfish

You will find some species of starfish on just about any sandy beach in the world. Many live in shallow water and can get stranded on the beach by a high tide. Others, such as the burrowing starfish and the sand star, live in the damp sand, and can be discovered after a little digging.

Starfish have hundreds of tiny, tube-like feet which give them a good grip on rocks and prey alike. The mouths of these strange, five-armed creatures are located in the centre of their underside. Starfish make a formidable predator, and they like to dine on whole worms and even molluscs, wrapping their arms around their prey to trap them. They force open mussel shells with

ABOVE *The marble sea star inhabits the coral reefs of Australia looking for molluscs as a food source. This brightly coloured sea star has five arms, which is the most common number, although some have as many as 45 arms.*

LEFT *The crown-of-thorns sea star, found in Australia, uses its arms and suction cups for locomotion, and for holding onto the coral where it denudes living polyps. This star is very destructive to coral reefs, since it is only the outer layer of the reef which is living.*

RIGHT *Colourful sea stars abound on rocky coasts and coral reefs looking for molluscs, their favourite food. They attach themselves to the bivalves and pry open the halves by maintaining a pressure greater than the bivalve muscles.*

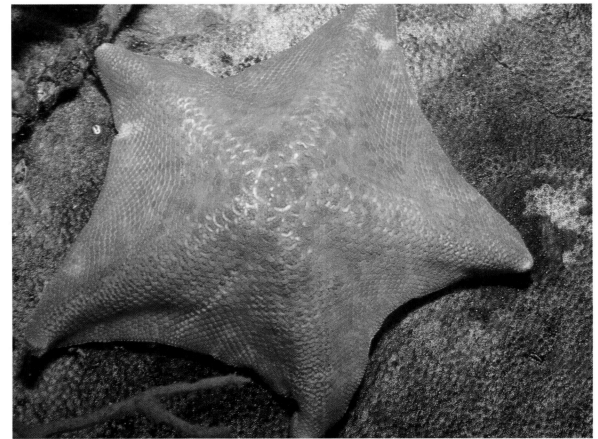

JELLYFISH

One of the strangest sights found on beaches around the world is a stranded jellyfish. It seems incredible that with their transparent, wobbly bodies these creatures are fierce and feared enemies of many marine animals. Yet as they float through the sea, or hang from rocks or seaweed, jellyfish are able to paralyse their prey with vicious stings from their tentacles.

Be careful not to touch a jellyfish you find on the shore: its sting can be very painful and in some parts of the world, fatal. But you can picture how the stranded creatures travel through the water: they pulsate the rims of their bell-shaped bodies, propelling themselves along with their tentacles flowing behind. Sometimes they are washed ashore, or stranded by the tide. These will dry out and die. Others may be trapped in rock pools and have to wait to be rescued by the tide.

The most dangerous jellyfish to man is the sea wasp, which lives in the warm waters of the Pacific Ocean. It has killed several swimmers off the Australian coast with its powerful paralysing sting. The longest these people have survived after being stung is 20 minutes.

The jellyfish swims by pulsating its bell. The mass keeps it afloat and sense organs keep it from swimming into deep water where there is no food. The jellyfish needs to remain towards the surface to secure its food.

LEFT *Sea stars are often found in tidal pools as well as areas close to the shore. They feed on mussels and clams.*

BELOW *The Portuguese man of war is related to corals, sea fans and jellyfish. Its long tentacles contain a highly toxic poison, as dangerous as a cobra's venom.*

their tube feet, then insert their stomachs to digest the creature, leaving behind an empty shell.

Starfish can grow back lost arms – even if they lose up to four of them. The tips of these arms are very sensitive to light, and help the starfish 'see' its way to safe, shady crevices, or to burrow down into the damp sand. There is no front and back to a starfish: any of its arms can lead the way.

Some starfish live deep under the sea, like the largest ever found, which measured 54½in (138cm) from tip to tip. Others can have as many as 50 arms. There are many varieties of this curious creature all around the world.

The human threat: pollution

Wander along the high tide mark when the sea is far out and you will usually find many pieces of debris. Some of it is litter left on the beach or thrown from the shore, and other objects have been discarded over the side of ships and washed to the shore.

The wonderful thing about Nature's debris is that it is reused again and again – as food or shelter for example. That line of debris will attract scavengers such as birds and crabs to pick out anything useful. Man leaves rubbish which takes far longer to disintegrate, if at all. Plastic bags in particular are a threat to the animals of the shore as they can get trapped in them and suffocate.

Many tons of oil are released into the sea, sometimes by accident, sometimes as an act of convenience. Bad instances often attract publicity as helpers try to rescue damaged birds, but if you spend long enough at a seashore, you are bound to come across small-scale examples of oil pollution yourself.

It can be argued that the very presence of tourists on the beach is a form of pollution, but you can do your best to ensure this is not the case. Try to leave the beach not as you found it, but slightly better, by removing litter and telling the authorities of any large scale pollution. That way future generations can also enjoy the beach.

The influence of the moon and the sun

An explanation of the tides and their relationship to the sun and moon is complex, but it is possible to generalize somewhat. Tides are caused by the gravitational pull of the moon and the sun, with the moon being the prime mover and the sun playing a lesser, but very important, role.

BELOW *The once idyllic Marshall Islands clearly suffer from the effects of pollution, as the shores of Majuro are buried under mountains of scrap metal.*

SPRING TIDES AND NEAP TIDES

This diagram shows the position of the earth, sun and moon for the highest and lowest tides of the month (known as spring and neap tides respectively). When the sun and moon are in direct line with the earth (resulting in new and full moons), their pull is combined, working together to form tides higher than normal. In the first and third quarter, the pull of the sun and moon work against one another, and the tide is lower than normal.

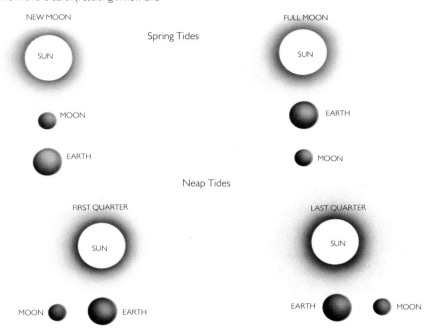

NEW MOON

Spring Tides

SUN

MOON

EARTH

FULL MOON

SUN

EARTH

MOON

Neap Tides

FIRST QUARTER

SUN

MOON   EARTH

LAST QUARTER

SUN

EARTH   MOON

There are two basic types of tides. Spring tides occur twice each month and denote the highest of all tides for the month. Their name has no relationship to the season but refers rather to how they appear to 'spring' upon the land. These tides occur several days after the moon is full and the same time after the moon is new. When the moon is full, the earth lies directly between the sun and the moon. When the moon is new, the moon and sun are in a direct line on the same side of the earth. At these times, their pull is combined and the tides are higher than normal.

The lowest tides, called neap tides, occur when the moon is in its first and third quarters, appearing to us as half moons in the sky. At these times, the moon and sun are at right angles to the earth so their effects as tide makers are balanced by each other's influence. Although this account holds true in general, tides from different parts of the ocean may interact with each other and produce extremely high or extremely low tides at other times.

Normal tides during the rest of each month are called flood tides and ebb tides – high and low tides in everyday terms. The easiest way to think

ABOVE *Here, the beach has a wide berm between the foreshore and the primary dune. This berm provides some of the sand used to make dunes.*

of tides is to imagine that the sun and moon cause the oceans to form bulges on each side of the earth. As the earth rotates on its axis, the water levels along the coastline rise and fall alternately. In most areas this phenomenon occurs twice a day at an exact, predetermined time. Local newspapers on the coast often say when high and low tides will be for days ahead. Tides occur in all parts of the world, but in the many areas where they are hardly visible, as in

Seashore Identifier

the case of the Mediterranean Sea, they do not happen on an exact timetable, nor do they occur even twice a day.

Many other factors affect the pulsations of tides on sea coasts throughout the world. The topography along the sea floor, the local offshore currents and irregularities of the coastline are all contributing factors of tidal movements along a coast. The tide originates in the ocean, and as it approaches the coast the slopes of the offshore sea-bed will affect the height of the tide. The combination of the shape of the shoreline with the tide can affect the height of the tide as much as the moon and sun.

The most dramatic example of this is the Bay of Fundy on the east coast of Canada where the tide's rise and fall may exceed 50 ft (15 m). The Bay of Fundy is a very long and narrow bay which receives so much tidal flow that the water has nowhere to go but up. As a contrast, the coast of Nova Scotia has a vertical tidal difference of about 6ft (1.8 m). Other places in the world are also famous for their dramatically high tides. There are points along the coast of England where the tides can range over 40 ft (12 m) between high and low tide. Similarly, the southeastern coast of Alaska has tides of 36 ft (11 m).

The tidal bore, associated with high tides, is one of the most fascinating phenomenons related to tidal change. When very large tides or those confined to a narrow bay or channel come in with a tremendous surge, the resulting noise sounds like the rumble of a distant train. The tidal bore occurs in the Bay of Fundy where the tide runs upriver on top of the water flowing downstream, sometimes reaching a height of 5 ft (1.5 m). The town of Moncton, New Brunswick, Canada, is a famous location for watching the bore, a phenomenon which also occurs in the Severn and Solway Rivers in Britain, the Amazon River in South America, Cook Inlet at Anchorage, Alaska, and Hangchow Bay in northern China.

Conversely, the Mediterranean Sea and the Tropics are locations which experience tides of only 1–2 ft (0.5 m). Tides such as these hardly affect intertidal life, in contrast to more temperate zones. There, the different water levels at different times of the day allow a variety of flora and fauna to survive at the sea's edge, depending on the plant or animal's water requirements.

Tides as transporters

Tides can transport large amounts of sea-bottom material, an indication of their energy. A tidal current of ½ mile (0.8 km) per hour will move sand along the bottom; 1 mile (1.6 km) an hour will move fine gravel; and a tidal current of 2½ miles (4 km) per hour will move coarse gravel up to 1in (2.5 cm) in diameter.

It is during the winter months that most changes to the shoreline are brought about. This is because winter storms usually have stronger waves that are closer together than those of summer. The distance between waves in summer means that as one wave washes the shore, much of the water sinks into the sand, permitting the next wave to enter the beach zone alone. In contrast, the quickness of the wave pattern in winter does not allow the prior wave to sink in, and so the returning water drags the finer sand back across the beach into the wave area, where it is deposited. These deposits take the form of long sand bars or ridges, which may also form underwater. These bars eventually grow large enough to help quiet the waves' assault on the beach.

BELOW *This wave is beginning to break where the sea bottom has slowed the lower portion of the wave. The crest continues at its original speed, falling forward into a mass of foaming water.*

Since only the finer material is drawn offshore during the winter weather, the heavier pebbles and shells are dropped back onto the beach. Your favourite beach will often be filled with coarse material if you visit in early spring – you might not even recognize it! As spring arrives, the action is reversed and the quieter waters begin to move the sand forward to the beach. By summer, the bars will have disappeared and the sand returned to its original structure. Even so, you may be able

ABOVE *This shows more serious beach erosion. The waves are washing into a tidal pool higher on the beach, but water is flowing out of the pool at a greater rate, carrying more sand grains below the foreshore.*

to see how the winter wave action has made the beach steeper as it removed the fine sand.

A general guideline for the slope of a beach is as follows: a sandy beach will have a slope of 9° or less; a beach that has a slope of 10° – 14° will be covered with coarse sand; and a beach that has a slope of 15° or more will be covered with gravel or shingle (a flat pebble).

High winds produce stormy seas. As the winds blow across the ocean surface, the particles of water rub against each other, causing a friction which sets the sea in motion in the same direction as the wind. As the surface water begins to move, the motion is transferred downwards. Intermittent winds create coarse waves, whereas ripples develop when the wind velocity is constant across the water's surface. The longer intermittent winds blow, and if they increase in velocity, the greater the likelihood that the size and intensity of the waves will develop into a serious storm. If the winds continue, the waves can begin to break and whitecaps (or white horses) are then formed.

Once the winds have died down, the whitecaps will disappear and the waves will become undu-

LEFT *This erosion design is caused by water receding from a wave higher up on the beach. Some sand is returned to the water by this process.*

THE JOURNEY OF A WAVE

Waves move in a circle. The crest of a wave moves horizontally in the direction that the wind is blowing, but beneath it, the water moves in the opposite direction, creating a circular motion. Waves passing under an object on the water's surface such as a gull or a piece of wood do not noticeably transport the bird or wood horizontally, but leave the object bobbing up and down. This indicates that a wave is a form of energy which travels through water, rather than moving, or transporting, the water itself. The same action can be seen with wind flowing across a grass field; the grass bends with the wind but does not physically move in the field.

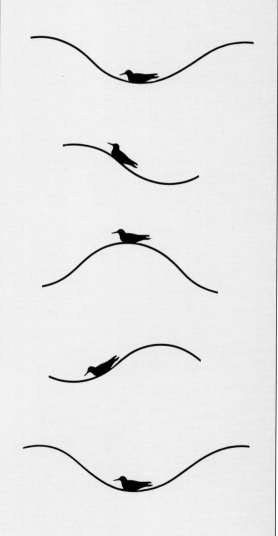

The diagrams above illustrate the manner in which the wave moves through the water, without displacing it or causing any forward movement. The bird bobs up and down on the waves, but is not transported from its original position.

lations called swells. These swells have the ability to travel hundreds of miles to crash onto an un-suspecting beach causing extensive damage. Swells are common in areas of the world where winds are forever sweeping across the water's surface: they are an everyday occurrence in waters north of Antarctica, for example, and often reach heights of 30 – 40 ft (9 – 12 m). It is shallow areas off the foreshore that cause a shoreline to be harmed. As a swell approaches the shore, its base is slowed by the friction of the sea bottom, but the crest continues toward the shore at its orig-inal speed; as the swell 'trips', it falls forward into a powerful breaking wave.

How sand is made

As you walk along a beach and gaze at the sand, reach down and scoop up a handful. When you separate the grains with your fingers, you are re-viewing the end product of possibly millions of years of work by nature. Most of these sand grains have reached the smallest size possible in the erosion process, bar becoming particles of silt or mud. Each grain will have a long history, begin-ning as rock, fractured by frost and roots of trees, ground fine by glacial movement, and finally fin-ished by the ocean waves. Blown to the sea from areas inland or carried by streams and rivers that empty into the ocean, all the accompanying minerals have long been broken away or dissolved by water.

When glaciers were at their most active (during the Pleistocene period which ended 12,000 years ago), they covered the northern section of North America, the northern portion of Europe and nor-

ABOVE *The tidal bore arrives at Moncton, New Brunswick twice daily. This is a small bore, and the river will quickly fill with water from the Bay of Fundy.*

RIGHT *Over thousands of years, the violence of the waves combined with the annual freezing and thawing of winter have formed this cave out of solid granite. The rocks surrounding the cave have been able to withstand the forces of nature.*

thern Asia. The ice masses were so thick that much of the sea water was consumed by glacial snow, reducing the ocean levels by 300ft (90m) or more. As the glaciers expanded and moved south, and then receded and advanced several times, they ground and scoured the surface of the earth. Large boulders were broken into smaller rocks; rocks were broken into pebbles; and some ma-terials were ground into sand and silt. The glaciers pushed this material into high piles or filled up depressions beneath the ice with it.

As these glaciers melted the ice water ran away in streams and rivers, and in the process, loose rock material was picked up by the stronger waters and tumbled towards the sea. This journey ground the rocks and pebbles into smaller particles, and once deposited in the sea, wave action reduced the particles even further, polishing the sand

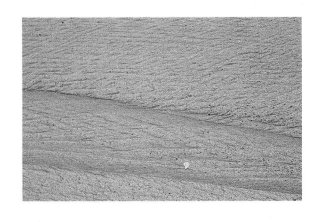

RIGHT *The ripples in this sand are caused by waves striking the shore at an angle to the beach.*

The Sandy Beaches

25

grains and rounding the rough edges. In total contrast to this, Arctic beaches have little or no sand because the ice build-up prevents a normal wave action, and so reduces the sea's ability to erode material on the sea-bed because there is insufficient movement of the water.

Older beaches are characterized by larger accumulations of material that has been ground to a finer texture. The ancient beaches along the Atlantic coast of North America, for example, still receive their material from the Appalachian mountain range, carried to the sea by the Susquehanna, Delaware and Hudson Rivers. The southern American beaches of the Atlantic do not have a large mountain range to supply raw material, and are composed mostly of pulverized shells and fragments of other marine skeletons.

The colour of sand depends upon what type of rock it is made of. White sand, which is very

ABOVE *A snow pond is also called a kettle pond because its bottom is in the form of the round bottom of a kettle. It is a freshwater pond but is located very close to the shoreline.*

BELOW *The mixture of hornblende and quartz sand in this picture is an isolated area of the beach; the remainder is quartz sand only.*

common, originates from quartz, seashells and coralline algae, an alga that develops a calcium shell which remains after the plant's death. The whitest and brightest sand is composed of this pulverized coral from the coralline algae, and this sand is formed only in tropical areas. Black sand comes from volcanic lava which has been eroded by the sea; St Vincent Island in the West Indies is a good example of this, fringed as it is with black sandy beaches.

The beaches of Tahiti are also a clear indication of the origins of different coloured sands. Dazzling white on the leeward side of the island, with sand formed from shell fragments and the powdered skeletons of marine life, the north side of the island has black sand beaches formed from an old lava flow. In North America, the grey-green sands of the Oregon and Washington coasts are caused by basalt deposits carried to the sea for over 100 miles (160 km) by the Columbia River.

The cliffs of Alum Bay on the Isle of Wight are made of tilted layers of sandstone and clay, tilted as if a layer cake had been picked up and set on its edge. These vertical rock layers are coloured by iron salts resulting in a variety of hues, which the eroding sand has revealed. Some of the beaches of Newfoundland are dark grey from the local slate, and in Nova Scotia, red beaches take their colour from the local sandstone.

In general, waterborne grains of sand are more rounded and smaller than grains found on the berm, or dune, areas and which have been deposited there by the winds. Water action rounds the sand's edges as the grains rub against each other, whereas windborne sand has sharper edges and is larger in size. Heavier grains are likely to be found on the upper beach area while the finer grains remain lower on the beach or in areas protected from strong winds. Similarly, larger and heavier pebbles are deposited higher on the beach than the lighter, smaller ones.

The moist intertidal sand is marked by beach wrack which is deposited by the high tide. Between the wrack and the water lies an area that is neither sea nor land, populated by tiny, primitive fauna and no flora whatsoever. The sand in the intertidal zone contains a space around each grain that is filled by water. No two grains of sand touch one another, and this provides enough space for minute animals to live. These tiny crea-

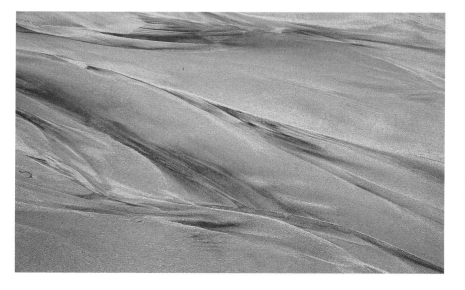

tures include worm larvae, nematode worms, rotifers and copepods. Molluscs bury into the wet sand and 'clam up' at low tide but become active feeders when the sand is covered by water, straining out the particles of food brought in by the waves and tides.

Flocks of shorebirds land on the intertidal zone when the wet sand is exposed, looking for food washed ashore by the sea. They seem to know just when and where to feed, coming back time and time again to the same location.

Pebble beaches have even fewer small animals and plants living beneath the surface because their delicate bodies cannot withstand the constant shifting of large objects which crush and grind, destroying most attempts to establish a life on the beach. Pebble beaches are no more permanent than sand ones, and waves can grind a pebble to sand in just one year. As the pebbles are reduced in size and washed into the sea, new ones are being deposited upon the beach.

A visitor returning to the same unprotected beach year after year will be amazed at the shifting of sands and pebbles by action of the waves and currents as they are driven against the beach by winter gales. Considerable amounts of money have been put into trying to reduce the effects of heavy seas on the beach sand, bringing in sand by the truckload, erecting pilings in the water, and building rock jetties that project far out into the surf. Nevertheless, people have not been able to harness the waves nor the winds that tear and rip at the shores from ocean storms; they can discourage major damage, but they can never

ABOVE LEFT *On this beach, the foreshore occupies the space between the water and the base of the primary dune. There is no well-defined berm on this beach.*

ABOVE RIGHT *A gravel beach has a steeper slope than a sandy beach. These pebbles are much the same as found on the shingle beaches of the French Riviera.*

control the severest of the winter gales.

Unprotected beaches are in a constant state of change because the sands are continually being eroded and replaced. The waves and currents draw the beach sand into deeper water, building a sand bar parallel to the beach. The next storm will smash the sand bar, rebuilding the beach line back to its original shape. Through all the turmoil, the bivalves, worms and other tiny animals in the wet sands remain, being able to adapt to this ever-changing world. This is amply demonstrated by the beach at Carmel, California. In the month of July, the beach is nearly 200ft (60m) wide. As autumn approaches, the waves tear at the beach sand until it has nearly vanished by mid-winter. The sand begins to rebuild in the spring and has fully recovered by the following July.

Another major factor in sand movement is the longshore current, hidden from view under the water just past the waves. This current is formed by waves striking a beach at an angle to the shoreline, and the water movement tends to move sand from one part of the beach to another, or even to a beach farther down the coast. Such currents are also responsible for forming sandspits, bars of sand with one end against the shore and the remainder extending into the water. Responsible in part for the changes to beaches and the destruction of property built too close to the sea, longshore currents have the power to move sand like a conveyor belt. Attempts to control these currents with jetties and other artificial devices have generally been unsuccessful.

THE ROCKY COAST

Imagine waves crashing against a rocky shore with spray flying high into the air, and small sea animals clinging tenaciously to the rocks dashed by waves, exposed to sunlight and drying air, and to rainstorms which wash away the salt. On northern shores, ice forms on the rocks making it even harder for the small animals to hang on. This is the hostile world of the rocky coast, whether a coast of granite rock resisting the waves or of soft stones that crumble and enable the sea to carve indentations into the coastline.

This type of coast is a sharp contrast to the sandy beach. Here more fauna and flora can easily be seen among the rocks, and offshore life on a rocky coast is quite different from that of gentler beaches because the water is generally colder in northern areas of the world.

Recreation along the rocky shores

The intertidal zones and the tidal pools join together to provide much of the recreational activity on these shores. Many people enjoy peering into the tidal pools to see what moves and what lives there, jumping from rock to rock over cracks and crevices in the hope of finding a new seaweed or a different animal that was swept upon the shore at high tide.

Power boats are popular along any sea coast, as are sailboats. The rocky coast appears to attract larger sailboats than the beach areas of the temperate zone, which are beautiful to watch from the rocks.

Standing on the rocks with the waves pounding below, it is easy to dream of the seafarers who sailed the seas long ago, and to imagine the difficulties they must have endured. Gales that drove ships aground, waves that washed sailors overboard into icy water, and fog that could swallow people up, never to be seen again.

When waters in the northern zones froze solid with ice, people would turn to seal hunting on the ice floes. Public outcry against the killing of seals has virtually eliminated this activity now, and today there are modern trawlers plying the

ABOVE *The plant and animal life found on rocky coasts has adapted to harsh conditions not encountered on sandy beaches, such as crashing waves, drying effects of the sun, and colder water.*

sea in search of fish, processing them and storing them in freezers before returning to port.

Visiting a rocky shore can be an exciting experience and you can often find more interesting creatures and plants in a small area than on a sandy beach. However, rocky shores can also be dangerous. Some rocks are slippery even without a covering of water, and you should always move slowly and carefully, checking that your next step is safe before proceeding.

Tennis shoes give a good grip. Only venture onto the rocks when the tide is on its way out –

MAKING A CLEAR-BOTTOMED BUCKET

A clear-bottomed bucket will allow you to study underwater life in rock pools and other places very easily. You will need a large plastic bucket with a flat base. Using a sharp knife (under adult supervision) cut a circle in the bottom about one inch (2.5cm) from the sides all round. Measure the inside diameter of the bucket, and have a piece of glass or rigid plastic cut to a diameter about an inch smaller – so that it will fit on the bottom of the bucket, resting on the ledge you have left. Fix the sheet in place with a silicone-based glue, making sure you have a good seal all around. Weigh the glass or plastic down until the glue has hardened. Now you can enjoy looking at underwater life as it is really lived!

THINGS TO DO

▶ Try to find all three main varieties of seaweed – brown, red and green – and look for differences between seaweeds within each group.

▶ Try to catch a limpet or whelk unawares and prise it off the rock – it is almost impossible. How do animals which feed on these creatures get at their prey?

LEFT *These rocks, situated high above the high tide, receive spray from the waves pounding the rocks below. As the water dries, salt deposits build up.*

never when it has turned. Some tides come in very fast and you could get trapped. Do not visit rocky shores alone, and always ensure that someone outside your party knows where you are going.

When walking among pools, try not to put your feet in the water as you may disturb a fish or other animal which has a nasty sting or bite. If you want to study the animal life in a pool, place a clear plastic container on the surface of the water, or take a glass-bottomed bucket. You will get an excellent view of what is going on without disturbing the inhabitants too much.

You may like to gather a few animals or sea-weeds for your marine aquarium (see Chapter 1, *The Sandy Beaches*), or just make a list of the many different kinds of creatures you find, and what they eat. Indeed, food is an interesting theme for a visit to any part of the seashore; you can try to discover what each animal eats, and which animals prey on it. The marvellous thing about nature is that these elements balance so that no one animal is safe from predators.

Intertidal zones along rocky coasts

Beneath the lowest tide is a world that is eternally wet, where constant exposure to air would kill the organisms living there. Just above the high water mark of the highest tide is a land that

BELOW *Here, the intertidal zoning can be seen clearly from the rocks. The dark band at the top is blue-green algae mixed with black marine lichens; periwinkles and barnacles share the next zone; and wrack and Irish moss are below them.*

is free of saltwater, and a constant exposure to water would kill any life there. Between the extremes lies a wealth of plants and animals that must adjust to both worlds. For most, it means a world of wetness. They need water to live and they shut tight against the world when stranded without water.

The area between the extremes of the tides is broken down into several different zones; each zone contains separate flora and fauna with only a minimum of overlap. The more tolerant an organism is to water or sunlight and air, the more it is able to move from zone to zone. Whatever zone a species occupies, it must be able to meet the shore's basic challenges: temperature variations, ice grinding on rocky surfaces, rain washing the salt away, and waves breaking with never-ending violence. Every plant or animal must build a defence mechanism to protect itself against these variations in its environment, or it will soon disappear. The compensation for all this effort is a food supply that is plentiful in a well-developed food chain. By adapting to these harsh conditions, the coastal species improve their chances of survival.

There are many ways to break down the tidal zones, which have led to some disagreement between scientists as to the zoning of certain species. A simple method would be to divide the zones into four areas – the splash zone; the high intertidal zone, which is under water 10 per cent of the time; the middle intertidal zone, which is under water 50 per cent of the time; and the lower tidal zone, which is under water 90 per cent of the time. Another system, as used below, is more descriptive but is not necessarily more accurate than the four zones mentioned above. In reality, there is more mixing of animal life between the zones than the layering implies, although plant life is accurately portrayed.

BLACK ZONE The black zone, or splash zone, is located just below dry land and just above the high tide. Contact with the sea is primarily through the spray of waves splashing from the rocks below. This intertidal zone derives its name from the colour of the covering on the rocks, which looks like a stain. It is in fact a living and breathing colony of blue-green algae, enormous numbers of them living in the spray from high tide.

LEFT This close-up shows the blue-green algae that live on the rocks in the splash zone.

PERIWINKLE ZONE Only the highest of spring tides are able to submerge this high intertidal zone. The chief inhabitant is a marine snail, the rough periwinkle, which is about twice the size of the small winkle and has a rough shell. This animal appears to be on the verge of evolving into a land creature because of the extended periods of time it is removed from water. Periwinkles have gills, which, as long as they are moist, enable them to breathe atmospheric air when on land. Additionally, they produce fully formed young from eggs that hatch inside the mother, which is a characteristic of most land snails. Periwinkles from this tidal zone move up to feed on the blue-green algae of the black zone. Using its radula, or raspy tongue, with its sharp little spikes, the periwinkle saws at the algae to loosen it from the rocks.

These plant-like organisms, related to bacteria, are among the oldest and most primitive of plant life. Each tiny algae plant is covered with a gelatinous (jelly-like) sheath which protects it from drying in the sun and air when the tide is low.

Algae grows in partnership with fungi to form lichens, which grow all round the world on rocks, trees and other surfaces, and are capable of surviving in very harsh conditions. On rocky shores you are likely to find yellow lichen right at the top of the black zone, with orange lichen below and further down black lichen. Each has adapted to survive with different amounts of exposure to light, spray, wind and so on.

Living in crevices among the lichen you may find the small winkle, which grows up to about ¼in (5mm). Of all winkles it is the most capable of surviving in exposed conditions.

RIGHT Periwinkles cling to the sheer cliff face.

BELOW The shells with pointed ends are dog whelks, with a periwinkle on the bottom left. The whelks eat mussels, barnacles and periwinkles.

THE BARNACLE ZONE The acorn barnacle predominates in this high intertidal zone, glueing itself securely to the rocks and feeding on minute organisms brought to it by the tide. The price these little animals pay for living in this zone is exposure to air twice a day for several hours at a time. They take the heaviest pounding from the waves, and at low tide, the hot sun beats down upon them during the summer months. Once cemented, the barnacle is stationary for life thus becoming an easy target for the dog whelks that feed upon them. The whelk is a marine snail that

The Rocky Coast

31

forces the barnacle shell open and consumes the soft tissue inside it.

While the rockweed zone below may be a haven for mussels, there may be as many mussels in the barnacle zone as there are barnacles. It is possible to find barnacles growing on the mussel shells since neither can move about after, as plankton, they settled upon a landing site. Mussels attach themselves to secure objects with byssus, a silky black thread spun out by the mussel when it first gains a foothold on a solid surface.

ROCKWEED ZONE This middle intertidal zone is a gentler shelter lying below the barnacle zone. It is less exposed to the air and spends a greater amount of time covered with water. Rockweed, a stout rubbery weed also known as sea wrack, abounds there. Sea wrack is a general term for a family of plants called wracks. The most common forms are channelled wrack, flat wrack, bladder wrack and knotted wrack. These plants can be most easily identified by the tiny bladders formed somewhere on the plant (different for each wrack plant) and are used by the plant to aid in floating upright when covered by salt water. As a contrast, common brown kelp, located beneath the wracks in deeper water, have no bladders as they are able to remain upright without them.

ABOVE *Shrimps occur in tide pools as well as the deeper waters of the sea. Tide pool shrimps, such as this one, are too small to be of commercial interest. They protect themselves from natural predators by hiding in rock crevices.*

LEFT *White barnacles and baby mussels cover the rocks by the water's edge at low tide.*

BARNACLES

Some barnacles such as those with feathery limbs are happy to set up home on any surface where they will find a supply of food. This includes the hulls of ships, where they build up and slow down the vessel. Barnacles can travel the world in this way — perhaps this is how the Australian littoral barnacle crossed the globe to invade British waters in 1945. Special anti-fouling paints are often used on hulls to fend off the barnacle, but unfortunately some of these kill off other creatures, too, and damage the environment. In 1990, the use of the most toxic paints was made illegal.

When you look along a rocky shore, there could be millions of barnacles in front of your eyes. Some Australian shores are populated by 120,000 barnacles to the square yard (metre).

A major predator of the barnacle is the dogwhelk, a gastropod which uses hard teeth on its hollow tongue to bite through the barnacle's shell. It then sucks the juicy meat up its tubes. On sheltered shores the dogwhelk's shell is thin and ridged with a small mouth. Rougher climes produce a thicker, smoother shell.

When the tide is out, the barnacles close their six plates to provide a protective wall around four smaller horizontal plates which fit tightly together, closing the shell. The open barnacles are no longer alive.

MUSSELS

Mussels are blue/black bivalve molluscs which eat plankton, the microscopic life forms that float through the sea. To get enough food, some mussels filter 10 gallons (4.5 litres) of water a day.

Some varieties of mussel are edible, and can be quite delicious, but they have to be prepared and cooked first. Put them in a bucket of fresh water with a couple of handfuls of oatmeal overnight. The oats should be eaten by the mussels which will get rid of any sand in their stomachs. Then they should be well scrubbed in running water. They can be boiled with onions for about 10 minutes. Any that do not easily open were dead before they were cooked and should be thrown away.

One variety of mussel found only off New Zealand is called the green-lipped mussel and is used to treat arthritis.

ABOVE Mussels are highly adaptable and can live totally underwater or be exposed to the sun and wind by tidal changes.

LEFT Mussels fasten themselves to the rocks by silken threads called byssus.

RIGHT *Rockweed, also known as wrack, completely covers the rock down to the low tide line. Irish moss can be seen in the background.*

ABOVE *The wrack or rockweed is attached to the rock with a holdfast. It has no roots.*

Limpets can be found firmly attached to rocks near the sea all around the world. They are easy to spot because seaweed cannot establish itself where they have colonized. You could be forgiven for thinking that they are permanently attached to the rock, but their lives are more active than that. Limpets are really the snails of rocky shores, with conical shells well designed for survival in the stormiest sea and for protection from the sharpest bird's beak.

Like other molluscs, the limpet has one sucker-like foot with which it attaches itself to the rock. It twists its body around, bringing the shell into the rock to get a tight seal for security and to prevent itself drying out at low tide. It occasionally crawls around on foraging trips up to 3ft (1m) away from its home base, always returning to the same spot. If it bumps into another limpet, each tries to force it's shell under the other's, exposing its vulnerable soft tissue and ensuring a rapid retreat — for a snail. Feeding usually takes place under water when the tide is in, but the limpet may graze for nourishment in moist and damp conditions.

You might be able to knock a limpet off its rock, in which case you can examine it closely through a magnifying glass. The mouth is on the opposite side to the foot, which has tiny tentacles between it and the shell.

Rockweeds provide shelter for mussels, common periwinkles, smooth periwinkles, tiny crabs and snails. The snails, or limpets, secure themselves primarily to rocks and remain stationary while exposed to sunlight and air. As the tide reappears, they move off to feed, always returning to the exact same location, 'home', as the tide drops.

The rockweed and other brown seaweeds living in this zone usually grow to a maximum of 6 – 7in (15–18cm) long, which protects them from drying out when exposed to sun and wind. At low tide, this seaweed often appears to be black and gives the appearance of being dead. However, it retains moisture and life, and once covered by the incoming tide will resume its normal appearance of shades of brown to slightly green.

BELOW *Here are two of the several different wracks found in the sea. The green wrack is bladder wrack and the brown wrack is channelled wrack.*

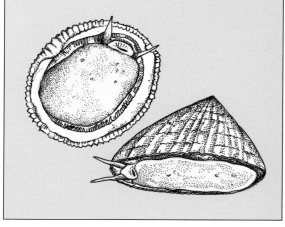

The common periwinkle may occasionally work its way to the periwinkle zone to feed on the lower portion of the algae from the black zone, while the smooth periwinkle cannot tolerate much air, so it never feeds on the blue-green algae. Both of these periwinkles lay their eggs and fertilize them in the water, and are highly dependent upon water to preserve their species.

Rockweed does not have a root system as found in land plants. The entire length of the rockweed

Seashore Identifier

draws nutrition from the water, serving the same purpose as the roots of land plants. The roots of the rockweed are called 'holdfasts', and their only purpose in life is to anchor the plant permanently to a rock.

IRISH MOSS ZONE This low intertidal area is only exposed to air and sunlight at the lowest of low tides, low ebb tide and neap tides. This area is crowded with red-brown Irish moss and the shiny-leafed sea lettuce. This flora mats the rocks and protects the fauna living here from the force of the waves, as well as predatory species intent upon a hearty meal. The Irish moss and sea lettuce provide a hiding place for the prey of crabs and starfish in particular. It is possible for both Irish moss and sea lettuce to exist in this zone alone.

THE LAMINARIAN ZONE This zone is named after plants called laminarias, and could just as well be called the kelp zone, the common name for laminarias. Not a true zone, it is only mentioned because at low tide the tops of the kelp are exposed to the air and sunshine. At this level, there

are some deeper holes where light has difficulty penetrating, and it is darker and much colder in these pools in the northern areas of the world. This laminarian zone is not found along all coastlines; it is only present where there is 7–8ft (2–2.5m), of water at low tide.

The laminarias belong to a group of brown algae, similar to the wracks found higher up in the tidal zone. This zone is populated by larger animals made up of crabs, urchins, starfish, anemones, sponges and an occasional jellyfish. There may also be larger fish swimming in the kelp.

Tidal pools on rocky coasts

Within the intertidal zone lies an area where pools of water exist between high tides. While these areas are small in volume compared to the entire shoreline, they provide special areas where life exists because water is constantly available. It is interesting to visit these parts of the coast to examine the variety of sea life which thrives in this environment.

Some portions of rocky coastlines are composed of cliffs where the intertidal zone is displayed on

BELOW *Two primitive animals which can be spotted in tidal pools are the sea urchin and sea anemone.*

solid, vertical rock. Other rocky areas begin low, as a sandy beach, with higher rocks found 50–60ft (15–18m) inland at low tide. These areas hold the tidal pools and become submerged as the tide rises. These pools provide a space for plant and animal life to cling to the surface of rocks. Delicate plants grow in the crevices, nearly undisturbed by the force of the waves, gently drifting to and fro and hiding tiny sea creatures.

Since the inhabitants of the pool are constantly beneath the water, life within a pool is more dynamic than that surrounding it. In the pool everything is partially exposed to the sun, wind and rain which dilutes the seawater, and it provides a perfect location for life which cannot tolerate being exposed to air. Nonetheless, pool life has problems of its own. Some of its animals perish from the lack of oxygen in the pool water if the tide returns too slowly, and under certain circumstances, the changes in salt content in the remaining water can play havoc with the life of animals since they are sensitive to it.

Sea anemones, sea urchins, limpets, sea stars

ABOVE *Sea urchins are common inhabitants of rocky tidal pools as well as the rocky shore beyond the breakers.*

(starfish) and chitons are common pool inhabitants, and sea lettuce, tiny rockweed and a few algae round out the flora. The common dark-green sea urchin is found in pools everywhere, curious creatures which can survive along rocky shores as well as in more sheltered spots protected from most predators by their bristling mass of spines.

Sea urchins produce large numbers of young, most of which are eaten in the plankton mass. However, enough survive so that huge swarms can be found in pools and crevices, along the shore, and in seaweed growing in subtidal water. Many adults may be found in traps set by fishermen. They move very slowly because they have no head and, since their shape is round, they have no front or back. Sea urchins are transported by reddish-brown tube feet which help draw them along like a sea star.

At times urchins reproduce in such numbers that the huge quantities are known as urchin plagues. It is not known why this occurs, but some theories suggest that a reduction in the number of fish that eat them has dramatically enhanced their ability to survive. Another theory is that a combination of mild, gentle weather and an abundance of food helps them multiply. There are also lean years in the urchin breeding cycle, however. Over-abundance of fish, a lack of food and large, mature urchins which indiscriminately eat anything, including their own offspring, mean that the young can only develop when the larger urchins die off.

Rock pools are easy to examine because you can stay in one place for a long time without being disturbed, and the creatures in the pool have nowhere to escape to. Pick a comfortable resting place where you can lie down (make sure you are not blocking the path of the sun) and give your eyes time to adjust to the darkness of the pool. You will find that what appear to be pebbles are camouflaged animals, and a piece of rock may turn out to be a lurking crab. Do not disturb the water surface for you will alarm the inhabitants and they will hide away again.

You might be surprised to find fish in your pool. They may have become trapped in the rock pool between tides but will be quite comfortable in the higher temperature of the water. Some

RIGHT *These tiny sea lettuce plants are growing on the bottom of a little tidal pool formed on the rocks. The fact that plants are growing here shows that this is a permanent pool.*

BELOW *The hermit crab never grows a shell, and spends most of its life hunting for a new home. As it grows, it constantly must seek a larger shelter for protection. It is not common to find hermit crabs on the beach, because they hide during the daytime.*

choose to spend a lot of time in pools or near the rock and have developed suckers to stop themselves being thrown around by the waves. The lumpsucker and the goby are two examples of this. Other fish lie flat on the bottom of the pool, camouflaged and ready to strike at their prey. The brown and green shanny is one of these – a fish capable of surviving for quite some time out of water, and sometimes found sheltering under boulders until the tide comes in. You might also find a sea scorpion, which changes colour as a form of camouflage.

Often, things are not what they seem in a rock pool: disguise is a way of life for many of the

creatures in it. Look carefully at any snail shells at the bottom of the pool. One could be the home of the hermit crab, which lives in empty winkle shells, moving to a larger home as it grows. You may catch the crab moving about as they are active during the day – their large pincers offer excellent protection.

The young edible crab is another likely resident of the rock pool. It usually hides under rocks or in crevices, but you may see the tip of a claw sticking out. This crab has a pinky-brown shell and moves offshore as it gets older.

One of the easiest animals to spot in a rock pool is the sea anemone, because it seeks out the sunniest parts of the pool where it can spread its tentacles towards the light. This strange creature has a tube-like body attached to the rock or a shell. It searches for food with its many tentacles, stinging crustaceans and other small organisms and pulling them into its open mouth. Some varieties of sea anemones are beautifully coloured – particularly in the tropics – while others blend easily into the background.

You may be very lucky and discover that there is an octopus trapped in the rock pool you are observing. These have a round oval body and eight arms covered with rows of suckers. They can change colour to blend in with the scenery and wait to grab unsuspecting fish and crabs that pass by. Octopuses can squirt out an inky screen to distract predators. The larger relatives of examples you might find, living off the Pacific coast, can grow to a span of more than 26ft (8m).

RIGHT Sea slugs feed on the poisonous tube anemone without harming themselves and retain the toxin for their own protection. Anemones are stationary animals and are, therefore, susceptible to molluscs which rasp away at their flesh.

BELOW LEFT The finger-like projectiles of the anemone come in different sizes and shapes but all are designed to stun the tiny fish it feeds upon. Some anemones will attach themselves to a shell occupied by a hermit crab; thus the anemone will be transported about the ocean floor.

LOBSTER FISHING

There is one occupation that remains much the way it was done in the past, and that is lobster fishing. Since lobsters and crayfish hide in rock crevices and move along the ocean floor, these shellfish are still caught by baited, submerged traps. Many lobstermen are carrying on a multi-generational family tradition, with as many as three generations on one lobster boat – the grandfather, father and the grandson all working together to bring in the day's catch.

Each lobsterman has his own distinctively marked buoy and as he sets out before dawn, he begins looking for his buoys; his pots may be located in the same area as five or six other lobstermen. He gaffes the rope connected to the buoy at the surface and the trap far below, and places the rope over a pulley to haul the trap into his boat. These water-logged traps made of wood, or wire; together with their rock weight, may each weigh up to 70lb (30kg). The traps must lie on the sea floor to entice the lobster to enter. If there is a lobster large enough to keep, the lobsterman will plug or band its claws to

A lobsterman working his trade along the shore. Lobster trap buoys can be seen around the boat.

protect the other lobsters in his tank and then refills the baitbag and drops the pot overboard, heading off for his next buoy. The lobsterman is an integral part of the shore because his buoys may be floating only 30–40ft (9–12m) from the rocks on shore.

This lobster is alert to any danger so it can slip into its home in the rock crevice.

Another sea creature that may become trapped in a rock pool off the Pacific is the sea slug, or nudibrachs, which is similar to a land slug: a mollusc without a shell. Some sea slugs eat anemones and use the swallowed stinging cells to catch new prey.

Prawns are another possible find in a rock pool, but you will need to keep your eyes peeled because they are transparent and move very fast if disturbed. A frightened prawn will dart rapidly backwards by opening its tail and flexing its body. Prawns have three pairs of walking legs and five pairs for swimming, so they are quite mobile in the bottom of the pool as they search for weed fragments and animal debris to eat.

Birds on rocky coasts

Many species of bird thrive on rocky coasts because their surroundings are such a bountiful source of food. Each tide washes in more tasty creatures, some of which become stranded on the rocks or drop their guard in their search for prey. Of course the sea itself holds a huge supply of fish, and some birds circle above it until they spot a target, then dive down towards it, completing the chase by swimming.

Insects, slugs, worms and snails are the chief food of the rock pipit, a small 6½in (17cm) brown/ black bird which nests in holes and crevices behind rocks. They can be seen picking over pieces of seaweed, looking for periwinkles and larvae.

Oystercatchers and turnstones can be found on rocky shores as well as sandy beaches, and are

ABOVE LEFT *The navanax sea slug grow up to four inches (10cm) in length, with many of the varieties maturing at less than four inches long. They are bottom feeders and spend their entire life in the quest for food.*

ABOVE RIGHT *Despite appearances, the shag will not build its nest on exposed cliff sites, but seeks a sheltered position in a crevice or cave. In the breeding period, the shag develops a short crest on its head. It is smaller than the great cormorant, with a shorter neck and longer bill.*

sometimes found alongside the purple sandpiper, another wader bird which breeds in the Arctic and flies south for part of the year. This is a stocky, brown and purplish bird with a white belly and a long, curving bill. It hunds for food along the shoreline, dodging the waves and occasionally hovering above them, waiting to pick off the crustaceans and shellfish on the reefs.

You may know eiderdown as the warm and light stuffing which man uses for duvets and sleeping bags. Off the rocky shore you may see its source: the eider duck. This is a large diving duck which nests on stony shores and takes its food (mainly mussels) from the rocky bottom of the shallow sea. The male has a white back with mainly black wings when in breeding plumage. The prized down is collected by man from nests, where the female has plucked her own breast to line the home and keep her eggs warm. The eider inhabits

Seashore Identifier

the northern coasts of Europe, Asia and North America.

Cormorants can be spotted on coasts of all the continents except South America. These large birds make an impressive sight, sometimes nesting in colonies of thousands. The cormorant is easy to spot as it is predominantly black, measures up to 36in (90cm) long and nests on exposed sites such as large rocks. It fishes for its food with well-timed dives into the sea, and then has to lie with its wings spread to dry out before the next hunting trip. Cormorants are ancient birds – one cormorant fossil is thought to be 100 million years old. They are also highly intelligent and in some countries fishermen train them to catch fish and return with them to their master – they are allowed to eat every fifth catch.

Seaweed

If you visit a rocky shore, you are bound to find some seaweed. This is a plant form also known as algae which does not have roots: it uses structures called holdfasts to grip the rock. Unlike most plants and trees it does not gather its nourishment from these root equivalents, but absorbs food through its whole surface.

ABOVE *The eider duck, whose down provides filling for bedding, is one of the most numerous sea ducks in the world.*

RIGHT *The enteromorpha is a bright green seaweed that frequents tidal pools. The fronds are shaped like simple tubes or straws. The seaweed grows at the lower level of the tidal zones.*

Seaweeds use light from the sun and carbon dioxide in the water for a process called photosynthesis, a by-product of which is oxygen – essential to keep other creatures alive, including man. Seaweed offers an excellent habitat for many sea and land creatures who use it for their protection and as a hunting ground for their own food.

There are thousands of kinds of seaweed, some of them tiny and others huge (the Californian

RIGHT *The considerable fishing skills of the cormorant have caused it to be used by fisherman in some countries to retrieve fish from the sea. Cormorants can be spotted on most coasts around the world. Its feathers are not waterproof, so it must dry off in the sun between meals.*

LEFT *Sand pipers feed on rocky shores as the tide rises, and can be seen darting to and fro to avoid the waves.*

giant kelp can grow 3ft (1m) in a day and may reach a length of 300ft (100m). It is so extensive and rich in food that the local sea-otters lie partially covered in it while they keep an eye out for sea-urchins, crustaceans and shellfish to eat.

Seaweeds fall into three main groups: brown, green and red. Each grows in certain zones, with green more distant from land or shore, brown nearer and on the shoreline, and red on and below the shoreline.

Brown seaweeds include varieties known as wrack and kelp, and actually come in a variety of colours (including, confusingly, green). They generally favour sheltered shores – so they can also be found in caves, rock pools and gullies.

Being farthest from the shoreline, green seaweeds have thicker cells walls so that they can retain the moisture needed to survive.

Red seaweeds come in more varieties than the browns and greens put together. They tend to grow in the most sheltered areas where the waves are at their weakest, and can sometimes be found growing under cover of brown seaweeds. Red seaweeds get their colour from certain pigments which absorb low-intensity blue-green light such

ABOVE *Green spongomorpha is a brightly coloured seaweed with sponge-like characteristics which grows in tidal pools along the rocky coasts.*

as that found in sheltered and underwater areas. Their true colours can best be seen underwater – perhaps by holding a snorkel mask on the surface to get a clear view.

Sponges

It is an animal or a plant? This question has perplexed many for centuries, as people have argued about that strange life form often found on rocky shores, the sponge. In 1825 the microscope revealed that sponges pump water through their bodies, and they were accepted as a very primitive form of animal life.

There are about 500 species of sponge, the simplest of which is a hollow body in which the central cavity is lined with cells which move around to create a current of water. This water contains the oxygen and food particles needed for the sponge to live. More advanced sponges are larger and have a more complicated structure as the body wall is folded, making more room for the cells which in turn bring in more food. Large sponges might pump 4.8 gallons (22 litres) of water through their bodies every day.

Sponges live on the sea-bed or attached to

LEFT Rockweed is the more common name for various wracks. It is associated with any wrack that is attached to rocks along a rocky coast.

LEFT The knotted wrack can live only on shores protected from heavy waves. Where it is able to live, it dominates the entire area. The plant can grow to the height of six feet (1.8m) or more.

BELOW The sponge is one of the simplest of the multicelled animals, being no more than a community of individual cells with no central nervous system.

BATH SPONGES

Most of the sponges we use in our bathrooms are artificially made, but it is still possible to buy natural sponges. Divers have harvested these for thousands of years, using them for washing and even padding helmets, as the Romans did. Most of the best of today's natural sponges are picked, trawled or dredged from the coast of Tunisia. They have to be treated to remove the living tissue, leaving us with the sponge skeleton to wash with.

COLOURFUL SPONGES

Many sponges are quite dull but some are truly spectacular. The blood-red sponge is red or orange and grows in encrustations up to 20in (50cm) across – so it is pretty easy to spot. The yellow boring sponge actually tunnels into limestone or chalky substances such as thick shells, leaving part of its body with a large hole to collect or eject water through.

ABOVE Sponges are often found living in kelp beds which shelter them from larger prey. Sea slugs feed on the sponges because they too live in the kelp beds.

LEFT There is no pain when a portion of a sponge is eaten by another life form because the sponge lacks a central nervous system. Sponges are found throughout the ocean floor where its food is located. They attach themselves firmly to rocks, and draw food from the surrounding water.

rocks near the shore. You may be able to spot some quite easily but others are more cleverly camouflaged, and may just look like a film on the surface of the rock. Those protected from strong currents grow delicate branches to search for food above. You may find skeletons of some varieties of soft coral and sea mat sponges washed up on shore. They are known collectively as dead man's fingers because their long, spindly bodies look like dead hands. Some sponges crumble when touched – for example the yellow or green breadcrumb sponge, which is often found encrusted on underwater rocks and stones.

The sea-orange is a remarkable sponge which sometimes grows on whelk shells occupied by hermit crabs. It provides the crab with excellent camouflage, and in return the crab carries the sponge to a series of feeding sites. Sometimes the sponge dissolves the shell it began life on and attaches itself directly to the crab. In fact most sponges have close relationships with other animals such as worms, crabs and even small fish which live on the surface or even in the water channels of a large sponge.

Seals

If you visit a secluded area of rocky coast where few humans stray, you might be lucky enough to find some seals on the rocks, or swimming among the waves.

There are more than 30 species of seal, each adapted to the environments they inhabit around the world. Common or harbour seals are found through much of the cold waters of the northern hemisphere, from Britain to Greenland and South Carolina in the Atlantic, and from Japan to the Soviet Union, and Alaska to as far south as Mexico in the Pacific.

When on land to breed these seals prefer sheltered spots near deep water, in which they catch their diet of fish and other creatures such as squids and crabs. Seals can look comically ungainly on rocks, shifting their blubbery bodies around quite clumsily. Once in the sea, however, their streamlined bodies are perfectly shaped for fast swimming with quick changes of direction as they spot and attack their prey.

The grey seal is less widely distributed, being found mainly around Britain although it can be

LEFT *Unlike other seals, the harbour seal will give birth on secluded beaches or rocky shores where the animal feels safe. The pup is born with very coarse, grey hair, which has saved the harbour seal from concentrated hunting.*

BELOW *The harbour seal was the most common seal along the northeastern coast of North America, and many places in that area, such as Seal Cove, Seal Rocks or Seal Island owe their names to the harbour seal.*

seen on both sides of the Atlantic. If often comes ashore for its breeding season just as the common seals depart for the deep sea with their pups, but it tolerates much rougher conditions than its relatives. The grey seal is slimmer, noisier and more aggressive than the common seal – if you see some in the distance, listen out for their choruses of hoots and moans.

The largest seals are elephant seals, which can measure 18ft (5.5 m) long and weigh more than three tonnes. They live anywhere between northern California and South Georgia in the sub-Antarctic.

Seals have three enemies: sharks and whales are more than a match for them in the water, and man has for centuries hunted the seal for its meat, oil and skin. There have been numerous campaigns against the culling of seals – particularly baby harp seals off the Atlantic coast of Canada. These are prized for their pure white skins, which start to discolour when the pup is ten days old. The performing seals trained to do various tricks in circuses and other places of entertainment are usually California sealions.

Other mammals you might be lucky enough to catch a glimpse of near a rocky shore are walruses and otters. Walruses are unusual in that they spend most of their time in groups of separate sexes, so a whole beach full of them might be entirely male. California has a flourishing population of sea otters, much to the annoyance of local fishermen who say the animal eats the shellfish that provide them with their livelihood.

BELOW A crowded guillemot colony. These are stub-winged birds that live and breed along rocky shores. The guillemot does not build a nest, but lays its single egg on the bare rock ledge.

Life on the cliffs

Life is hard on cliffs, because they are so exposed and vulnerable to the elements. However, one major benefit they offer is that man rarely intrudes on the cliff face, and this isolation allows creatures to live relatively undisturbed lives within easy reach of an excellent source of food: the sea.

If you visit a cliff site never get too near the cliff edge – a gust of wind or sudden subsidence could

Auk is a general term for a type of marine diving bird which lives in the northern hemisphere. Apart from auks, razorbills, puffins and guillemots are included in this family. Its equivalent place in the southern hemisphere is taken up by the penguin.

A razorbill on a cliff ledge. These birds will often nest among guillemot colonies. It was once hunted for its feathers, which depleted its numbers. Now a protected species, the razorbill population is increasing. Because of their stumpy wings they find it difficult to become airborne when the sea is flat and there are no waves to help fling them aloft. They have no problem flying from a rocky cliff.

put you in serious danger of falling down onto the rock. Try to find a safe spot where you can look along the side of the cliff face, rather than down onto it.

The ledges and crevices of cliffs make excellent nesting sites for birds. As with other bird sites, never remove eggs from nests – not only is it cruel, in many countries it is illegal. The guillemot, part of the auk family, only needs simple accommodation because it spends most of its time fishing underwater. Guillemots nest together in large groups – packed in shoulder to shoulder sitting on their pear-shaped eggs. When the little chicks are 2-3 weeks old, they simply jump out into the air and learn very fast how to fly and swim.

Puffins dig nests in soft soil, often on the grassy slopes of cliff tops on rocky islands. They also have been known to take over rabbit burrows.

ABOVE *Puffins may be seen on the northern and western coasts of Europe. Unlike other auks, puffins only take their young to sea when they are fully grown. They dig nests in the ground and raise their young in groups. These birds are often caught in the nets of fishermen as they dive and swim for fish. When disturbed, the puffin will make a sound resembling a growl.*

These birds live throughout the northern and central Atlantic, and some spend the winter as far south as the Mediterranean. A stocky bird with a distinctive triangular beak and red legs, the puffin catches most of its food underwater.

The presence of birds on a cliff, even only for the weeks of breeding and hatching, has a permanent effect on the ecology of the area. This is because bird droppings (guano) make excellent manure in which plant life thrives. If you look carefully at the vegetation on a cliff you may notice how much taller the plants near the bottom are. This is because falling droppings have landed near them. The thrift, or sea pink, is one sea plant that loves cliffs and produces beautiful pink flowers when it blooms. By pushing their roots into the soil, plants such as this help to prevent soil erosion.

Formation of rocky shores

Inland from the rocky shores, many uplands are composed of hard surface rock which furnishes little sediment for the shore. Because of the underlying rock foundation, there has been little erosion to fill the coves and bays with sand. One of the primary sources of sand build-up is the run-off of the thin crust of soil from the surrounding landscape, carried to the sea by rivers and large streams.

In areas where the underlying rock is composed of softer material, much more sediment reaches the sea from inland areas. Alternating freezing and thawing helps to break down this soft rock, and the currents of freshwater streams and rivers further continue to erode the rock pieces into finer particles as they wend their way to the shore.

Where there is no broad beach to buffer the assault of waves on a shoreline, the tidal action will strip the shore to basic rock. On a rocky coast, there is no rejuvenation of beaches as there would be on a more resilient beach, because there is no extra sand for the waves to work with. Even so, a rocky coast still needs sand to fill in and smooth out the sea bottom and the crevices between the rocks.

The contour of any rocky coast is highly dependant upon the composition of the rock and how well that rock can resist the wave action. Basalt and granite tend to resist strongly, and form a buffer zone. The softer rocks, such as sandstone, erode much faster, because they are worn down by wind and rain as well as by the waves. These sedimentary rocks erode to the point that a bay or cove is formed.

The south coast of England at Dover is composed of chalk, which is so soft that it is helpless in the face of constant wave erosion. These chalk cliffs and other types of limestone readily dissolve in water, and standing water or fresh water dripping through the rock can dissolve the limestone

CLIFF EROSION

When waves smash into rocky cliffs, they form a cut line in the cliff and a slope of rock debris at the water's edge. This debris will be picked up by the waves which hurl the chips and pebbles against the rocks to further erode the cliff face, speeding the destructive process. On the whole, a wave will throw materials straight up in the air, and as cracks form in the rock, water and air are forced into these crevices with such force as to break off larger slabs of the cliff, undermining the wall. The top-heavy wall soon crashes into the waves and the cliff moves inland. Waves can smash into a rocky cliff at a force equal to 20 tons per square yard, so these walls of stone can offer temporary resistance at best.

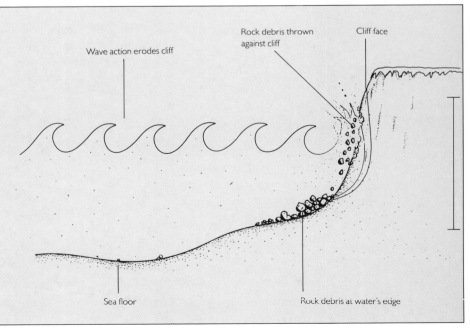

Wave action erodes cliff

Rock debris thrown against cliff

Cliff face

Sea floor

Rock debris at water's edge

to form tiny coves and grottoes, further weakening the pillars of stone. As the chalk falls to the sea, the waves sweep it sea-ward thus exposing more of the cliff to water action.

Ancient granite is exposed at Land's End, Cornwall, England, where wave action and rock falls have gradually worn away the cliffs. Waves have torn apart the granite at fracture lines in the rock, leaving a coast line of rock rubble with buttresses of stronger rock, which will continue to resist the waves for a long time to come. This same action is taking place along the New Brunswick coast of Canada and the rocky coast of Maine in North America. The basalt cliffs of Nova Scotia, Canada, are also being worn away in much the same manner as the granite cliffs described above.

Rocky coasts were formed primarily by glacial action, and there has not been enough time since the last ice age for the sea to break down these rocks and to form particles of sand: hence the lack of sandy beaches in these areas. Remember that the sea has only had 12,000 years to work on the rock formations, and there is only a thin crust of soil covering the inland rocks waiting to be washed to the sea.

Different formations among the rocks

Somewhere along a rocky coast there will be a thunder hole, a natural chasm created by the forces of the ocean. Large waves rush into the crevice and, having nowhere to go, will shoot straight up into the air, creating a thunderous clap and a cloud of sea spray. Waves have cut out a U-shaped crevice through solid rock to produce this unusual occurrence.

Because of the fracture designs in much granite, it is possible to have waves impact on one area of a cliff with no visible effect on adjacent areas. Storm waves, together with annual freezing and thawing, can break off chunks of granite and thereby form a large cave in an apparently solid wall of rock. The freezing and thawing fractures the rocks, but the storm waves are the real force that excavates the cave and moves the rocks into deeper water. Until you can actually see the results of the awesome power of the waves, it is difficult to believe water alone can move rocks that weigh thousands of pounds/kilograms from deep inside a cave to the open edge of the sea.

Standing on a rocky beach, it is possible to hear the clicking sound of rocks rolling as the waves reach the shore. The incoming wave picks up the small stones and pushes them up to the top of the wave action. As the wave recedes to make way for the next wave, the undertow of the water pulls the rocks back down the forebeach to await the next incoming wave. Each time the rocks roll up and down the incline of the beach and click together, small chips are broken off. The constant action of the waves repeated over and over again can break a group of stones down into sand within a year. Once the chips are produced, the remaining stones and gravel constantly roll over the chip until the sharp edges are worn to rounded corners and the entire grain takes the smooth shape of river stone. This grain will continue to be reduced in size until all the softer minerals attached to it are worn away, and the harder quartz or feldspar remains.

BELOW *Here, water is entering rock fissures, gradually breaking this granite into smaller pieces.*

Glacial effects on the shoreline

While inland mountains rose and fell hundreds of millions of years ago, molten materials rose up from beneath their surface and solidified into granite rock. Some of the lava erupted through the earth's crust and formed basalt columns. In other areas, a build-up of mud, sand and lime, often thousands of feet/metres thick hardened into shale, sandstone and limestone.

The earth was still restless and continued to heave and recede, placing more molten material on top of the old rock. Rocks that were formed by layering, with one on top of another, were suddenly forced on edge by the enormous pressures from inside the earth. As the glaciers arrived with the recurring ice ages from the north, they receded, and then moved south again. The earth's crust buckled beneath the awesome weight of ice and debris caused by the bottomless glaciers, which resulted in a considerable amount of destruction.

BELOW *This bay lies between New Brunswick and Maine in North America. The bay is now at low tide; when the Bay of Fundy fills, the water here will rise about 38 ft (11.5 m).*

The glaciers scoured the rocky surfaces, pushing huge land masses in front of the advancing ice. Loose rocks were caught on the underside, scraping the earth's crust to form river valleys and fjords, and much of the debris was deposited far from the world's current shorelines. Rocks the ice could not master were still affected as the freezing and thawing process, together with the upswelling from pressures below, developed fissure lines in these ancient landforms.

As the glaciers finally receded around 12,000 years ago, all the accumulated ice began to melt and the oceans began to rise, covering much of the land that was tilted towards the sea. With the punishing weight lifted from the earth's crust, the land began to return to its original elevation. Proof of the land rising can be seen in areas of the world where marine deposits have been found many miles inland, together with evidence of ancient shorelines above present-day sea levels. The waves and tides began working on the various rock structures along our current seashores.

There is one area along the coast of New Brunswick, Canada, where the waves have cut out flowerpots along the shore. These designs have been photographed so extensively that probably everyone has seen a picture of one of these pillars. The action started 300 million years ago, give or take a year or two. Rivers and heavy rainstorms carried sand, gravel, mud and boulders from higher ground inland to these deposits. This material was deposited on a flat area in deep layers where thousands of tons of weight exerted pressure on the deposits and pressed them into solid rock. The pebbles and boulders were cemented into place by hardened silt, with a result known as a conglomerate. In addition, scattered through this conglomerate are layers of sandstone hardened by the same methods.

The earth's crust began to go through a period of upheaval and this region was uplifted, twisted and tilted. Long vertical cracks formed in the soft stone, and the surface was eventually broken into large blocks. Water entered these cracks and froze, thus widening the cracks even farther. Waves lapped at the vertical cracks and the softer stone was eroded, leaving a pillar of rock just offshore. As time passed, the old pillars have been completely broken down and new ones formed closer to shore. The process will continue as long as the

conglomerate remains. Fundy National Park is home to these pillars, being located toward the head of the Bay of Fundy. This entire area of Canada contains large deposits of red sandstone which turn the waters of the Bay of Fundy a rusty red colour.

The shoreline around the world has remained approximately in its current position over the last 4,000 years – not long enough really to work on the hard rocks along the coast. The waves have had a considerable effect on some of the softer rocks along the shoreline, eroding the weaker sandstones, limestones and conglomerates.

Ice build-up on rocks along the shore

Winter plays havoc with the seashore, particularly in northern areas prone to ice. The wave action, together with the weight of the ice, grinds and scrapes, dislodging the fauna and flora clinging tenaciously to the rocks, and ice moving on the tide scrapes and saws at the salt grasses growing in salt marshes.

Once ice has scraped life from the surface of the rocks, the plants and animals cannot just re-populate the scoured area. The bare rock has to follow the evolutionary process as if the surface had never been exposed to salt water, first developing a surface film of bacteria and diatoms, and then allowing a growth of hydroids to form. Later, an algae growth will set the rock surface with the proper base, leaving the area ready for repopulation by rockweed. The total process can take three or four years.

The effects of fog

A silent, muffling fog presses on the shore along the rocky cliffs overlooking the ocean. A strange silence takes over as birds take roost and insects settle on the bushes and tall grasses. An occasional gull may fly by, its call strangely loud in the eerie silence.

The fog occurs when a cold ocean current surfaces against air warmed by the sun. Evaporation from the water's surface condenses into tiny particles forming clouds which lie against the earth's surface. The water particles settle on the trees and bushes outlining the silken strands of cobwebs where no cobwebs seemed to exist before. Walking along safely above the cliffs, the sound of the incoming waves crashing against the unseen rocks below accentuates the powerful force of the sea.

The monotone sound of a lighthouse fog horn can often be heard booming out, as an inability to see any distance sharpens the hearing senses, but fog absorbs most of the earthly noises. Depending upon conditions, the fog can settle in for many hours, overnight, or even for day after day until it becomes a way of life, and clear weather becomes the exception. While fog does not affect the flora and fauna of the seashore, it does affect the movement of people both along the shore and on the water. Sophisticated electronics can guide ships safely through the fog, but people using smaller boats and vehicles must be very cautious when navigating during this time.

BELOW Although most ships now depend on electronics to guide them through the fog, no shore line is complete without a lighthouse.

THE PROTECTING DUNES

The dunes towering above the sandy beach, made from the finest sand particles and powdered by the wind, provide a barrier between the sea, the salt marshes and the land behind. Sand being driven by the ceaseless winds building one grain upon the other blows across the beach until caught by the grasses. Growing to heights of 100 ft (30 m) and more only to be knocked backwards by the wind, dunes can move 10 – 15 ft (3 – 4.5 m) per year towards the salt marsh. If the dune is not stopped, it will smother the wetlands and kill all life in the marshes.

The beach is the first defence in stopping the sea from invading far inland, but it provides only a minimum of protection from the waves, so the dune acts as a natural backup system. The more securely the dunes are anchored with plant life, the more difficulty the sea will have in eroding the dune fortress.

There is usually an area above high tide where the sand remains dry, caressed by water only at the highest tides. This finely ground and polished material is swept away by shore winds and transformed into dunes. Depending upon the quantity of the sand available and the topography behind the beach area, the dunes can extend as far as a mile or two (1 – 3 km) behind the shore.

When sand is accumulated in sufficient quanti-

ties along a shoreline, dune building can take place. The lack of available sand is the reason there are few dunes along a rocky coast, although in time, as waves break up the rocks, there will be more dunes along all our coasts.

Dunes form from a clump of beach grass or a piece of driftwood that causes the wind to slow and deposit sand around the obstacle. Once a small pile is formed, more sand is caught, and soon the mound is elevated and takes on the characteristics of a foredune, the dunes immediately behind the beach. (These are sometimes called primary dunes.)

The mounds are usually formed with a long sloping face on the side of the prevailing wind and a short steep drop on the lee side. In most instances, the prevailing winds will come from offshore so the long sloping face is behind the beach, facing the water.

Dune sand granules are smaller than beach sand because this finer sand is easier for the wind to move from the berm and foreshore in front of the dune. The surface of the dune sand becomes rougher the longer the sand remains on the dune because of the treatment by the wind. As the wind blows across the beach, it picks up grains of sand. When the wind strikes the face of the dune the grains of sand also strike the face of the dune dislodging more grains into the air which are transported by the winds. This action roughens the grains that were originally smoothed by the waves.

For the most part dunes resemble sandy deserts, yet they can hold moisture beneath their dry surface. Unfortunately the dry zone extends deep enough into the dune to discourage most plant and animal life. Some troughs between the mounds of sand may resemble a boggy area, particularly if some silt and clay material has been mixed with the sand. This material will hold moisture on the surface whereas sand will permit moisture to pass through into the dune.

There is a food chain associated with dune life, but the sparse area does not afford much of a variety. Mice and rabbits may live in the dune if

BELOW *Pine trees, such as pitch pines, are the first trees to grow on a dune when the nutrients are adequate. These will be followed later by the hardwoods, primarily oak.*

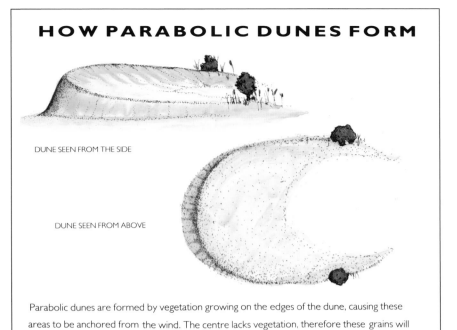

HOW PARABOLIC DUNES FORM

DUNE SEEN FROM THE SIDE

DUNE SEEN FROM ABOVE

Parabolic dunes are formed by vegetation growing on the edges of the dune, causing these areas to be anchored from the wind. The centre lacks vegetation, therefore these grains will be blown behind, causing a shift in location.

grasses are present, as will a select number of insects which feed upon the beach grasses. Small hawks take advantage of the sparse vegetation to search for the rodents residing in the grasses.

Different types of stable dunes

Coastal dunes come in a variety of sizes and shapes and are found from Australia and New Zealand to the coasts of Europe. Dunes are scattered around Great Britain and in countries along the Mediterranean. Both coasts of Central and North America, along the Gulf of Mexico, and the desert coast of Peru all sport dunes.

Foredunes rise up to 10 ft (3 m) behind the beach. These foredunes generally do not accumulate sand higher than this because they are affected so strongly by sea breezes; any excess sand would be blown inland to form additional dunes. The line of dunes behind the foredunes can grow higher since the initial wind velocity has already been blocked, permitting additional accumulations of sand.

U-shaped dunes exist with the open end towards the beach, assuming that the prevailing winds blow from that direction. Other types include crescentic dunes, which have a steep slope located away from the beach, traverse dune ridges and longitudinal dunes. The foredunes and U-shaped dunes are the most common types on most of the coastlines, however, with the wind

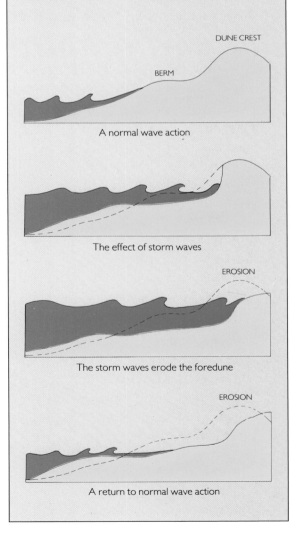

THE EFFECT OF WINDS, HURRICANES AND HIGH TIDES

The wind plays the most important role in shaping the dune system along a beach, but it can also be threatened by the unusually high tides and hurricane force winds that occur several times each year.

Storm waves have the ability to level a beach, reducing the size of the berm and increasing the slope of the foreshore. It can pound a beach so relentlessly that the beach disappears entirely, the foredunes, or primary dunes, carried away by the sea as their bases are eroded and the tops collapse.

If the dune system has sufficient depth along the shore, the primary dunes can stem the most destructive effects of the waves and the barrier dunes can contain the remaining energy.

DUNE CREST

BERM

A normal wave action

The effect of storm waves

EROSION

The storm waves erode the foredune

EROSION

A return to normal wave action

and rise high above the beach, so preventing water from flooding flat regions behind the dunes. They are usually located behind the foredunes and may rise to 100 ft (30 m) above the beach. Barrier dunes develop because of the strength of the prevailing winds originating from the ocean, which blow over large quantities of sand. Each beach and dune area has separate characteristics, and it is possible for a dune system to have two or more rows of barrier dunes, with enough sand and space, each one behind the other. Barrier dunes must have some reason for stopping, some obstacle or a lack of sand, otherwise they become travelling dunes.

Migrating dunes

Some dunes will be carried inland by the wind as long as there is no obstacle blocking its forward progress. These dunes may travel at the rate of 10 – 15 ft (3 – 4.5 m) per year and can travel several miles from the beach.

Winds striking the face of a dune will continue to build the dune higher and higher. When the crest of the dune reaches a height where the steep leeward slope cannot support its weight, the crest slides down the steep rear slope to the bottom. The sand accumulates again, increasing the height until the crest repeats its slide down the steep slope to the leeside, and so the dune inches farther inland.

Accomplishing such a task as this requires a huge quantity of sand, particularly when new

direction and its velocity in relationship to the beach being the deciding factors in the type of dune formed.

The U-shaped dune is the most interesting in its development. This dune begins as an oval, with beach grasses playing one of the two leading roles in its development as marram grass establishes itself on the flanks of the dune. This helps anchor the two outer sections, and as the wind blows against the dune it erodes the middle section which is unprotected by vegetation. Thus, the parabolic dune is sculptured by the wind eroding the centre section.

Barrier dunes is the term used for the dunes that provide the secondary defence behind the beach. These dunes can be parabolic, traverse or longitudinal depending upon wind movement,

foredunes are being developed next to the berm. A wonderful interaction of wave, tide and wind takes place to accomplish the feat of moving tons of sand from the sea to the dune crest. The wind is unable to transport the sand until waves and high tide move the sand up high on the beach. The wind must dry the top of the wet sand and be able to pick up the lighter particles, moving them to the berm where they can dry out thoroughly. Then the constant velocity of the wind loosens these grains and carries them to the dune area.

Human interference with the dunes

On an undisturbed beach, nature has a way of developing the shoreline, but the destruction of even a small area of dune grass by man can give the wind enough advantage to pick up the loose sand. If neighbouring dunes are covered rapidly enough that their dune grasses are smothered with sand, they will suffocate and die, and more sand will be moved.

In defence of human interference, nature can cause problems with the dune grasses. It is interesting to note that the grasses will die from the lack of new sand being supplied to the dune, as the nutrients become exhausted after a few years. Mankind can stabilize dune areas, but at a very high cost. Beach grass must be grown in a protected environment and then transplanted by hand onto the bare dunes. Since the first 6 in (2 cm) or so of dune sand lacks moisture, the

LEFT *The wind can blow sand over roads in sufficient amounts that periodically, the roadway requires clearing.*

BELOW LEFT *This dune is being moved by winds blowing from right to left, nearly covering the trees.*

BELOW *Where the sand is available, winds can form travelling dunes large enough to engulf buildings.*

planting takes place during the rainy season, or sufficient moisture must be added. In several years, the replanted grasses will stabilize the area and begin to control wind erosion.

The settlers at Provincetown, on the tip of Cape Cod, were guilty of cutting all the trees and permitting their cattle to graze on the dunes, destroying the vegetation. They were rewarded by having the winds recapture the sand, burying houses. People walking the streets of the town felt the sting of flying sand.

The American writer Henry David Thoreau wrote in 1849 about this experience, 'Nevertheless, natives of Provincetown assured me that they could walk in the middle of the road without trouble even in slippers, for they had learned how to put their feet down and lift them up without taking in any sand.' According to John Hayes in his book, *The Atlantic Shore*, Thoreau was to have said, 'This was the town where in some pictures the person of the inhabitants are not drawn below the ankles, so much being suposed to be buried in the sand.'

Once stabilized with the introduction of new grass, nature can begin its process once more. As the tops of the grass die in the autumn of each year and the plant loses a portion of its root system during the year, the grains of sand are mixed with the humus provided from the living plants. This change in dune composition provides nutrients for other plants and bushes begin to grow. The accumulated effect of these nutrients will eventually support the growth of certain species of bushes and trees.

Dune sands do not shift when it rains or when dew holds the grains together, preventing their separation by the winds. Very little sand is moved at night because of the dew, and dunes are stable against the rains because the seepage taking place through the dunes prevents run-off and erosion.

The dunes themselves are much like miniature hills shaped with ridges and valleys each of which has a different plant life. If the bottom of the dunes are close enough to the water table below, seeds from moisture-loving plants may germinate, and along with the additional plant life comes a variety of mice, rabbits and toads.

In many communities along the sandy coast, the dune system plays an essential role in de-

fending homes inland; once the sea has swallowed the dunes, houses are totally vulnerable to the force of the incoming waters and winds. As building takes place closer and closer to the water's edge, these areas have now become the premium properties to own. Their new owners are depending on the marram grass to keep the dunes together in the face of strong storms.

Flowers and grasses

All around the world, sand dunes owe their development and survival to one plant: marram grass. This is a colonizing plant which thrives in

ABOVE AND OPPOSITE *The aptly-named sea oat and sand burr (opposite) are among the plant life that can be seen on a well-established dune.*

BELOW *Dune grass will continue to grow as long as the plant leaves are exposed above the sand to air and sunlight. The roots grow downward towards water, anchoring the dune sand and providing shelter for other plant growth.*

THINGS TO DO

▶ Finding animal tracks in the dunes is fascinating. Look out for the tiny marks of a bird and the larger indentations a rabbit makes. Try to discover where the animal was going and why – does it live here, and what does it eat?

Crow tracks mark the bird's passage across the dunes.

▶ Try to identify the different kinds of grass along the dune, which will tell you how developed it is. If you find marram grass, it is quite young, and if there is a profusion of other varieties, this is a well-established dune.

The varied plant life on the dune indicates that it is well established. The plants at the bottom of the dune are nearer the water table and will differ from those at the top, whose roots dig deep down in the sand to reach the water supply.

BELOW *The common tern is one of the birds which benefits from the conditions on the dunes.*

At night this moisture rises nearer the surface, towards the spreading layers of the roots.

Other plants which grow in the dune include sea rocket, saltwort, sea beet, and sea couch grass and lyme grass – all with creeping root systems which provide a good grip to survive heavy winds. When these and other plants die, they decompose and provide nutrients for a new generation of plants: and thus the thick dune vegetation evolves. Eventually the marram grass, which paved the way for all this life, disappears because it is best suited to bare sand habitat and cannot compete with the new plants and lichens of the developed dune.

Animal life

Plant life supports animal life. Insects come to live on the plants and flies breed in rotting vegetation. This offers a supply of food to spiders – who in turn may be preyed upon by sand lizards and birds. Rabbits may start to browse along the dune looking for food (and their droppings contribute further to solidifying the dune surface). Eventually they will live in burrows bored into the moist sand, and eat the roots of the established plants. Birds such as the common tern scrape out shallow nests in which to lay their sandy-coloured – and therefore camouflaged – eggs. You may also see ringed plovers, oystercatchers and black-headed gulls.

the top dry sand as long as its long roots can find moisture. As it grows, these roots explore deeper soil, stabilizing the sand dune in the process and making it less likely to be blown away in a storm. At ground level marram grass spreads quickly and can cover as much as 30 ft (9 m) in a year. This also brings stability to the dune and provides opportunities for other plants to gather and prosper.

As sand is blown over the grass, totally covering parts of the original plant, the vegetation responds by developing new leaves that will grow above the surface, and root stalks that probe deeper into the heart of the dune. In areas where the dune has been cut by the wind, you might see a cross section of these roots growing ever-deeper. If you dig a little way into the sand, you will find that however much the sun has heated the surface, a little way down the sand is cool and moist.

THE FRINGING CORAL REEFS

ringing coral reefs grow in warm ocean currents just offshore, and act as buffers to protect the tiny particles of sand which collectively make up the beach. In the Tropics, reefs are the first line of defence against the regions' severe storms. They help to protect fragile flora and fauna of the beaches, dunes and mangrove forests from the harsh lashings of the waves.

Together with the barrier reefs and atolls, coral reefs provide countless hours of leisure time investigating the beautiful underwater world which inhabits these areas. They harbour some of the most unusual animal and plant life, as well as most of the colourful fish species along the shore.

Fringing reefs lie quite close to the water's surface, perhaps 150 ft (45 m) underwater at the most; in some places, they can be as shallow as 4–5 ft (1–2 m). These are ideal for exploring using a mask, fins and snorkel, or the more elaborate scuba equipment.

There are three types of coral reefs – fringing, barrier and atoll – but it is the fringing reefs which lie just off the shore, protecting the shore line. Fringing reefs are characterized by spreading laterally and continuously from the land in shallow, inshore waters.

Recent research into the origins of reefs suggests that fringing reefs are the origins of all three types of reef. Drilling revealed coral deposits thousands of feet below the surface of some barrier reefs and atolls. Since coral cannot live this

ABOVE *A vase sponge washed ashore on a shore built from a fringing reef.*

OPPOSITE *Elkhorn coral is one of the tallest corals on the reef, and one of the most popular with collectors.*

far below the surface of the ocean, the implication is that the barrier reefs and atolls really began as fringing reefs millions of years ago. The settling process of the earth's crust was slow enough to permit the coral builders to maintain their position just below the surface of the water, making it possible actually to build a coral reef 4,000 ft (1,200 m) thick over a million-year time span.

If the coral continued to build but the crust of the earth stopped dropping, exposure to the surface air would eventually kill the reef builders. Once this happened, a combination of coral sand and ocean debris would quickly fill in the reef. As gulls and other shore birds began to use the small bit of land, their droppings would fertilize an otherwise sterile sand. With the arrival of windborne seeds, plants would begin to grow, forming a new extension of land, or perhaps an island or cay.

LEFT *This rocky shore is composed of stones made from the calcium bodies of animals living on the fringing reef.*

RIGHT *Reefs, with time, become fertile land where plant life flourishes.*

CORAL REEFS OF THE WORLD

There is nowhere in the tropical zone where all three types of reefs are found together. No atolls are located in the Atlantic Ocean, with only a few fringing reefs found off the coasts of Florida, Central America and Brazil. Many more are located along the Red Sea and the Persian Gulf, and they surround the country of Sri Lanka in the Indian Ocean. Reefs extend from the African coastline of Mozambique and Tanzania and along the island shores of Madagascar. They are situated along the coasts of Sumatra and Surabaya in the Java Sea, along the coast of Australia off the Great Sandy Desert, in the northern Philippines between the Philippine Trench and the shore, and finally in the Bismark Archipelago along the Bismark Sea.

LEFT *During the day, moon coral fold up their tentacles and hide, as illustrated in this photograph. As twilight approaches, the feathery tentacles emerge to feed on plankton, which also become active at night.*

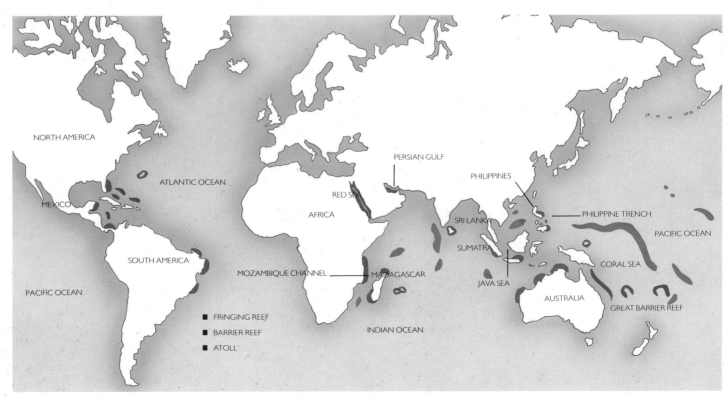

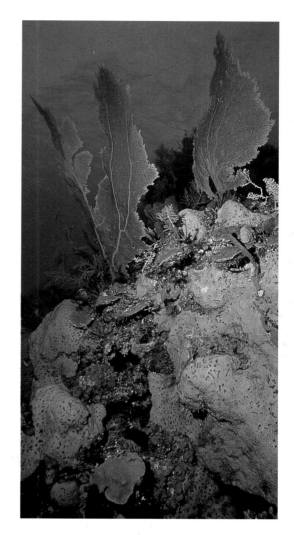

LEFT Pillar coral takes its name from its finger-like, or 'pillar' shapes. Although very small in diameter, this coral joins to build larger coral structures.

RIGHT Sea fan with orange sponges. The sponge does not contribute to the growth of the reef.

BELOW Soft corals, such as this orange tube coral, come in a variety of shapes and colours which attract the eye. They are not the real reef builders, but provide external decoration to the ever-growing reef.

Fringing reef

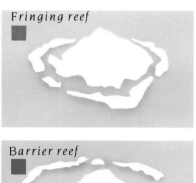

Barrier reef

Atoll

LEFT *This beautiful specimen is known as the sea fan.*

RIGHT *Antler coral grows upright where most coral stay close to the reef.*

Animal or plant?

The term 'coral' is used for both the animal itself and the cement-like substance it manufactures to build the outer shell of its home. For many years, scientists believed coral was a plant, but in the early 1700s naturalists discovered that coral was really an animal.

A very simple organism, coral is tiny, an almost transparent and jelly-like substance enclosed in a tube with an opening at one end. This opening serves as both a mouth to the animal and a means to excrete wastes. The edge of the mouth

BELOW *This close-up shows a section of brain coral, inhabited by small fish which clean out the material in the crevices of the coral.*

is covered with tiny tentacles, called polyps, a name which comes from Greek and means 'many footed'. Polyp corals live on tiny plankton separated from the water by its tentacles as ocean currents flow across millions of these tiny animals. Those same plankton are the food source for some giant whales and the largest creature in the sea, the whale shark.

Soft coral also live on these reefs, and their skeletons contribute to the reef formation, but the real reef builders are the boulder-like corals such as the brain coral. A single family of brain coral may very well build a skeleton 15 ft (4.5 m) in diameter and equally high, weighing several tons. The more common elkhorn and staghorn coral are built upon these boulder-like structures.

The taller-growing elkhorn, staghorn or pillar corals can reach heights of over 20 ft (6 m) and up to 10 ft (3 m) in diameter. These unusual corals are very popular with divers.

Coral reproduction and growth

Coral polyps reproduce either by eggs or by budding. The egg-laying polyps are hermaphrodites, capable of producing both sperm and eggs at specific times. The sperm and eggs are expelled into the sea where they develop as free-floating animals in the plankton. They then swim to an

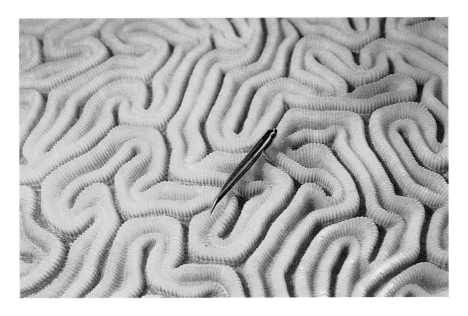

acceptable site where they settle down to lead a life like their parent. The budding process does not require eggs and sperm; the coral simply grows a bud on its body, which becomes a new creature. These new coral polyps build an exoskeleton and, like their parents, produce buds, a reproduction process which enlarges the coral mass with increasing rapidity.

Stationary throughout their lives, coral extract calcium carbonate from the water to form their external skeleton of limestone. As polyps die, the soft portions of their body decay, leaving the casing alongside thousands of other polyps, who are repeating the process growing beside and on the old skeletons.

Countries that are far away from the Tropics are deprived of this reef builder. Those within them, including America, are blessed with reefs. In the United States, there are a small number paralleling the Florida Keys. As a matter of fact, some of the Keys themselves are the remains of dead reefs whose builders lived in a warm sea 1,000 or more years ago.

Fringing reefs usually expand towards the sea, as polyps like to be exposed to the severest waves and heavy winds. The seaward side of the reef is where fresh salt water brings food in a constant supply, while the shore side of the reef is building up deposits of coral sand and debris, thus lacking a healthy habitat for coral growth. Coral is no different from other animals – they cannot survive if silt and sand cover them.

This animal has built structures under the ocean that dwarf the best and largest works of people. Coral reefs cover approximately 70 million miles^2 (112.5 km^2) of the sea floor, the greatest, and best known, of which is the Great Barrier Reef off the northeast coast of Australia. It has an average under sea height of 500 ft (152.5 m) and extends over 1,200 miles (1,920 km) along the coast.

BELOW *This piece of rose coral is feeding, extending its polyps to catch bits of food floating by.*

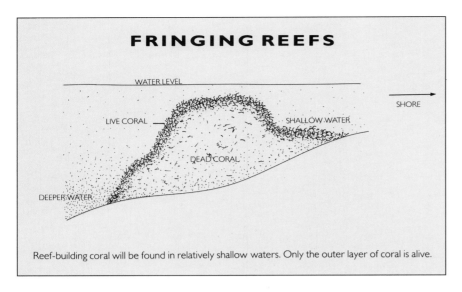

FRINGING REEFS

WATER LEVEL

SHORE

LIVE CORAL

SHALLOW WATER

DEAD CORAL

DEEPER WATER

Reef-building coral will be found in relatively shallow waters. Only the outer layer of coral is alive.

Sunlight is critical to the tiny polyp, as polyps have algae living within their tissue. In this symbiotic relationship, the polyp is dependent upon the algae to remove its wastes, including carbon dioxide, and the algae requires the coral to live in shallow water to provide the essential ingredient of sunlight. It is for this reason that reef coral are rarely found below a depth of 150 ft (46 m).

Human impact on the reefs

Collectors play a very destructive role as regards both the coral and the animals that live in the reefs. Collecting and selling the colourful fish is

Coral's environmental requirements

There are some 2,500 different species of coral polyps, out of which some 650 are reef builders. There are many other hard and soft corals throughout the world's oceans, but they are not builders. Reef-building coral have special requirements necessary for survival. They are found in clear, sun-lit tropical waters where the temperature does not drop below 70°F (21°C). Since these creatures are immobile, their demand for clean water is based on their inability to handle the silt found in dirtier water, and these conditions are only met in a belt around the earth's girth bounded by latitudes 30°N and 30°S of the Equator.

ABOVE *A piece of dead coral has washed up on the beach.*

LEFT *This pillar coral is one that grows upright, like the elkhorn and the antler corals.*

big business, and there does not appear to be any limits on the number of fish collected. Divers who break off pieces of the coral to take home as mementoes of their first dive can destroy in moments what took years to build. At present no action appears to have been taken to prevent further destruction.

Chemical pollution of the sea water is also lethal. It can kill an entire reef if the marine life cannot live in that environment, particularly if too much silt is carried to the reef and smothers the polyps. Life on the reefs does not have the ability to withstand pollution in the way it is assumed ocean waters offshore can.

As the daily routine of life goes on, so does the build-up of sediment along the reef flats, which some day will extend the shore outward from its present location. As long as the reef remains alive, it will protect this new land build-up from being reclaimed by the sea.

The reef's natural enemies

Living alongside the builders of the reefs are their destroyers: the sulphur sponge which dissolves the calcareous rock; molluscs who tunnel into the dead coral; and worms, who use their strong biting jaws to eat into it, weakening the structure and providing an opportunity for the pounding waves to break pieces off. Parrotfish also scrape the surface of the coral with their beak-like jaws, feeding on the algae growing on the dead coral and leaving gashes in the coral surface. After digesting the algae, the parrotfish return the scrapings to the coral floor in the form of sand.

The normal destruction of the fringing reef causes a sandy accumulation which slopes quickly from the top of the reef to great depths seaward of the reef. This slope causes waves to break over the reef and protects the shoreline from the constant pounding that is characteristic of other parts of the coastline, while the sandy accumulation gradually finds its way to the shore side of the reef.

The shallow water formed between the reef and the sandy beach provides a sheltered home for sea animals and plant life, but they are not as extensive as you would expect. The slower-moving water between the reef and the shore permits the sand particles suspended in the saltwater to settle to the shallow bottom, adding a minute layer of sediment each year. Hurricane winds, pounding high waves against the seaward side of the fringing reef, may deposit several inches of sediment on the offshore flats during a single storm. Over millions of years, this sediment will form limestone rock, but in the short term the layers of sediment in the shallows block the passage of oxygen to the roots of grasses and other plant life. The permanent animal life is similarly restricted to fewer species and less variety than is available at the reef. Often the flora and fauna are covered with a dusting of ground coral, which clouds the saltwater if walked on.

Night brings the larger predators from the depths beyond the seaward edge of the protecting reef. The sea becomes alive with these hunters, together with the creatures that remained hidden in the reef crevices during the daylight hours, searching for their daily food. From small shrimp to sponges and spiny lobsters, sea turtles

EXPLORING CORAL REEFS

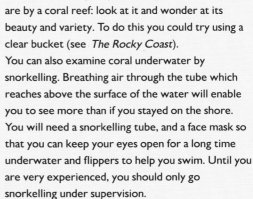

▶ There is really only one thing to do when you are by a coral reef: look at it and wonder at its beauty and variety. To do this you could try using a clear bucket (see *The Rocky Coast*).

You can also examine coral underwater by snorkelling. Breathing air through the tube which reaches above the surface of the water will enable you to see more than if you stayed on the shore. You will need a snorkelling tube, and a face mask so that you can keep your eyes open for a long time underwater and flippers to help you swim. Until you are very experienced, you should only go snorkelling under supervision.

▶ There are now some underwater coral reserves where corals are protected from the damage done by chemicals or careless fishermen. If there is one in the area, you should visit it. You may be able to purchase pieces of dead coral as souvenirs here, too.

LEFT Brain coral is one of the coral that will grow into boulders. It is credited with building the main structure of a reef.

BELOW Orange tube coral, one of the soft corals that become a part of the fringing reef.

and larger fish, all are hunters and all but the largest are hunted. As daylight approaches, or as the ebb tide draws near, there is an orderly retreat back to the lairs that provide a safe haven for the hunters and where they await the return of darkness.

THE SALT MARSHES

Salt marshes can form anywhere along the shore where conditions are correct for their survival. Some marshes are located at the mouths of rivers and large streams or along bays and deltas formed by large rivers. The barrier dunes defend the fragile marshes from the intruding storms that threaten both the shoreline and its living creatures.

If the protecting barriers are removed, the sandy beach is eroded by ocean currents running along the shore. Onshore winds may blow the fine, loose sand into the marsh, thereby burying and smothering the marsh plants and animals. If the marsh is exposed again as the travelling dune passes over this area and the dry sand is carried away by the wind and wave action, some of the dead marsh can also be eroded, since there will no longer be live roots to bind the soil.

The following spring there is no renewal of freshwater plants and the trees die because they cannot survive the salt environment. The saltwater claims a victory over the land and extends the size of the salt marsh.

The next step is for salt grass to migrate into this new section of marsh. The soil silt is still being deposited by the creeks and small streams, while the tide is gently flowing into the area depositing its sandy silt over the dead marsh grass. The salt marsh grows in elevation, and the stronger flowing streams begin to deposit silt beyond the beach. The marsh expands towards the sea, and even though it is battered by the waves, it more often than not makes headway.

Further gains by the marshes can come with a sand bar, formed by wave action grinding rock into sand and then depositing it. Until this happens, the silt-ladened water holds the fine particles far out in the quiet, deep water when they will finally settle on the bottom. A sand bar will cause the particles to settle earlier, thus building up the mouth of the stream into a delta. Once the accumulated deposits make the water sufficiently shallow, the marsh will expand into this area, and the grass will begin to root.

In a few hundred years, a large part of an original cove can be filled in in this manner, reshaping the cove. The boundaries of the salt marshes change, still reaching as far inland as the tide can go, and extending as close to the sea as the plants can stand. Many times, mud flats form between the marsh and the sea because grasses cannot live in a muddy environment.

One important factor in the development of a marsh is that the force of the waves is lost prior to the water reaching the salt flats. A common

LEFT *An egret preens its feathers in the everglades.*

BELOW *Observing the length of salt grass will indicate the location of the water source. Grass will be taller nearer the water.*

loaded with all the silt the water can carry. By dropping enough muddy silt to raise the elevation of the marsh so that it is no longer covered by saltwater, a river can eventually turn a salt marsh back into a freshwater swamp. This phenomenon occurs only where a large stream or river is involved in the development of a marsh.

Many coastal marshes exist where there are no flowing freshwater streams. Here, the sea is the sole influence on the growth of the marsh, and the beach and dunes protect it from the onslaught of the waves.

Salt marshes are the product of land erosion, and in areas on both the north Atlantic coast and the south and southeast coasts of England, which are sinking, the marshes need continually to be covered by new sediment equal to the rate of coastal sinking. If they are not, the marsh will be destroyed by becoming covered with salt-water for too long in each tidal change, hence killing the plants and animals living there. Strangely enough, the salt content of the soil would become so high that the plants would perish. Regular flushings by salt-ladened water keep the content low enough to permit plants and animals to live in this environment.

Human influence on the salt marshes

Some marshes are destroyed simply because they fill with silt, and the soil, being very rich in nutrients, is excellent for farming. But man tends to fill in the marshland with rubble and create roads, homes, offices and holiday housing. This method of land reclamation does not permit an equal amount of new marsh to be developed, with an eventual consequence of wildlife loss that is as yet unknown.

In England's Fens in the eastern part of the country, the salt marshes and peat bogs were barely above sea level in the 17th century. The Duke of Bedford hired a Dutch engineer, Cornelius Vermuyden, to convert the wetlands into agricultural lands, straightening rivers to increase the flow and reduce flooding. Small canals were dug

ABOVE *The dune in the background offers protection from the wind and waves for this salt marsh.*

thread existing with all salt marshes is the fact that the marsh is protected against the fury of the sea in all but the highest of tides and the strongest of winds. A marsh needs the gentle flushing action that occurs naturally with the change in tides.

The velocity of water is greater during a rising tide than it is in a falling tide, and faster flowing water carries more sediment than slower moving water. Thus the incoming tide carries more sand and silt into the marsh area than the outgoing tide can remove. Tides obviously cannot build a marsh elevated above high tide level, but a river can during flood waters when its waters are to carry water into the rivers and sluice gates were installed to block the tides from returning. However, when the peat dried out, it contracted by as much as 10 ft (3 m) causing much flooding from the sea. Windmills were first employed to pump out water, replaced now by diesel and electrical pumps. The reclaimed Fens yielded 115,000 acres of some of the most fertile land in England.

The beach and the dune areas are the first line of defence against severe storms, but the marsh provides a crucial buffer against the harsh effects of the waves. Wave damage occurs at its worst at the point where the waves break, and the shallow nature of the marshes forces the waves to expend the balance of their energy on the marsh, saving whatever lies behind the marsh. Persons destroying the salt marshes may be harming our assets close to the shore.

The tidal pools located in a salt marsh have a variety of plant and animal life very different from those of a tidal pool on a rocky coast. It is usually less varied and colourful than that of the rock pools. Clams generally live on the bottom of the pool, with small fish swimming about in the water with a few varieties of shrimp.

Every marsh the world over has worms as one of its primary inhabitants. While they vary somewhat in shape and colour, they all perform the same function. The lugworm is more interesting than most, digging a U-shaped burrow which has one end for taking in food, and a tail end for depositing excrement. Lugworms digest large volumes of muddy sand to extract organic matter, so they are found mainly in tidal flats. It is one of the few worms to have a burrow design other than a straight line into the soil.

The intertidal zone of the salt marsh

The intertidal zones occur in the salt marshes too. Unlike the dramatic rocky coast, very few of the marsh animals live in a dual world. Molluscs, worms and crustaceans belong to the aquatic group that lives near low tide and buries in the mud when exposed to sunshine and air. Most of the remaining animal life is terrestrial and simply evacuates the tidal area when the water level is rising. Some of the insects survive underwater for a short time by remaining motionless and using very little oxygen.

ABOVE *Tidal pools in salt marshes contain tiny animal life the same as tidal pools on a rock-bound coast. The life is not as varied as in a rock tidal pool.*

70

THE GROWTH OF THE MARSHES

Many marshes began as freshwater swamps with only a small obstruction separating the fresh from the salt waters. The salt grasses die in the autumn and form a mat of peat. The quiet invasion of tidal water twice a day drops silt suspended in the water, and this silt fills in around the decaying marsh grasses, increasing the elevation of the salt marsh by about 1 ft (.3 m) every 100 years. The freshwater swamp on the other side of the obstruction becomes covered with trees which shade the ground, permitting little plant growth. Erosion from the adjacent hillsides, the primary source of extra soil, is not enough to keep up with the increased elevation of the marsh, and one day a heavy storm at sea sends huge waves pounding the beaches at spring tide. The combination of an extra high tide with the wind-driven waves permits the seawater finally to break through the flimsy dam and invade the freshwater swamp.

Grasses are more suited to this type of tidal zone than animals. The shortest salt grasses need higher ground where the tide cannot reach them. A fine-stemmed marsh grass lives in the area of the high tide. In most parts of the world it is cut as hay for cattle. As we move towards low tide, the marsh grass becomes taller and coarser until the mud flats are reached between the marsh and the sea. No plants grow on this lowest portion of the intertidal zone but certain molluscs, worms and crustaceans survive here, as well as at the edge of the marsh.

The salt marsh supports a large number of economically important species of shellfish and fish. Some of these are only born in the marsh, others live their entire lives there. Some live and spawn in the sea, but the young come to the marsh to mature. Certain fish come into the marsh system to spawn, and the young return to the sea to mature, whereas others pass through this area to spawn in freshwater and return to the sea; their young develop in freshwater and move on to the salt estuaries before swimming to the sea.

Tidal creeks meander around the salt marshes through banks of peat deposited by the rotting stems and roots of marsh grass. The head waters of tidal creeks may be a freshwater pond or series of ponds, or the source may be marsh ponds. In the spring, fish from the sea will migrate through these streams to lay their eggs, and migrating waterfowl feed upon the creek banks and seek security from the marsh ponds. The water dislodges particles of decomposed peat which are then carried to the sea where they settle and enrich the shallow waters along the coast.

The salt marsh is an area rich in nutrition, and plays a vital role in the lives of many organisms, even though some of them spend only a short time in the marshes. In providing nutrients to coastal waters, the marshes act as a nursery for the beginning of the food chain, and the current pollution and filling-in of salt marshes and wetlands are eliminating a natural filtering system that is essential for purifying water.

The genus Spartina

Spartina is the genus of marsh grasses that grows throughout the world. Individual species differ in each country but the grasses look similar and all serve the same purpose: to hold the mud and silt that has accumulated in the marshes and to trap additional mud to form higher ground. Plants that can survive with their roots soaked in salt water, such as these, are called halophytes.

What characteristics does the *Spartina* grass have that permits it to live in this environment

LIFE IN THE SALT MARSHES

► Study the creatures in the salt marsh and try to discover if they live here all the time or are just passing through.
► Push a spade or shovel down and see all the life under the surface!

THINGS TO DO

This great blue heron can be seen walking through the tidal pools in the marsh looking for small fish.

when other plants die? It has a unique membrane that filters out most of the salt from the water taken in by its roots. Any salt that does manage to seep through this membrane is excreted through the leaves by a glandular back-up system. When the tide begins to cover the leaves of the *Spartina* plant, this glandular back-up system shuts down, thus preventing the plant from being drowned in salt water. The extra oxygen the plant requires is taken in by its glandular system.

Spartina grasses have been recorded as producing high yields of hay to be used for animal feed. This yield is better than an average rice field and is equal to the best hay-producing fields. What is more, the marsh grass does not cost anything to produce. But the real value of the plant lies in its nutritional content when it dies. As the plant falls to the mud, bacteria breaks down into a nutritional soup, food for marine life in the marsh as well as food for ocean dwellers. Some of the material is swept out to sea on the ebb tides, and many species of marine life flood into the marsh to feed on this organic material.

THE MANGROVE SWAMPS

The mangroves rule the sheltered shores, building land where there is no land. Their intertwining roots catch broken shells and bits of debris brought in by the tide, and they have established themselves so successfully that no other plant can threaten their dominance. The mangrove swamps, like the salt marshes, are land builders which prevent the eroding shores being swept away by the constant action of the waves.

The mangrove varieties

There are 46 known species of mangrove that inhabit the tropical areas throughout the world, and of these 46, there are two that stand above the rest. The red mangrove is the most easily and often recognized, while the black mangrove's roots, 1 in (2.5 cm) or so in diameter, run horizontally under the water sending up breathing

ABOVE *Red mangrove growing at the water's edge.*

roots above the mud. These roots perform the same function as the aerial roots of the red mangrove – to supply sufficient oxygen to the plant for its survival.

The green world of the mangrove is most often seen in the shallow coves and bay areas of the Tropics, where the warmth of the sun and the water are in balance for accelerated growth. The youngest plants are found closest to the open water, or furthest from shore, and are most often the red mangrove. The black mangrove fills in behind the red, both in the shallower water as well as on the land. This is just as well, because the roots of the black mangrove do not have the same ability to trap silt and debris.

The mangrove so dominates the shoreline that it has been able to eliminate nearly all competing plants from its areas of predominance. The same species live along the coast of tropical West

Africa and the extreme southeast coast of the United States, and this wide distribution is a tribute to the buoyancy of the seed pods and the ability of the ocean currents to flow in an orderly fashion. Where did the plant grow initially? It probably originated along the West African shores where the plants unwittingly used the Equatorial currents to transport their seeds worldwide. Further distribution of seed pods from the west coast of North America has led to plants being discovered on the islands of Fiji and Tonga, on Christmas Island, and on Krakatoa after it was destroyed in 1883 by volcanic eruptions. The mangrove is a wanderer throughout the tropical zones of the world.

Once considered a shore plant, it is likely that fierce competition for space with other plants and the struggle to survive genetically helped to develop its ability to survive in salt water millions of years ago. Scientists have classified the mangrove as belonging to the highest group of plants, called spermatophytes, or seed bearers. Seed-bearing plants have traditionally belonged to the classification of land plants, and the mangrove is a classic example of a land plant that has moved to water.

Over a period of 20–30 years, the mangrove plants mature into trees. This forest can withstand the battering of heavy surf, and only the strongest of hurricanes will cause severe damage. The root structure has evolved to prevent the uprooting of the trees in a violent storm, and although the tops are subject to the loss of limbs and bark they are rarely destroyed. These plants are survivors, withstanding all but the most severe beating by nature.

Anyone walking into a mangrove forest will experience the mysterious beauty of massive and gnarled trunks, of roots overlapping each other in a tangle too difficult to walk through, and of a green canopy overhead blocking all direct sunlight, permitting only diffused light to reach the soil below. A splash can be heard beside the narrow path, but the thick forest does not permit you to see what has caused it.

ABOVE *This scarlet ibis is found in the Tropics around mangrove swamps.*

The inhabitants of the swamps

The mangrove plant is the only major plant in the swamp, and all other plant and animal life is bound to it. While the forest is patiently building soil beneath its root system, the mangrove's arching roots are home to many different animals and fish.

Bivalves cling to roots, and periwinkles live on the plants near the high tide mark. Crabs thrive in the mud, feeding on the rich organic matter accumulated by the plants and helping to aerate the heavy mud, which is so deficient in oxygen. The mangrove has to breathe through aerial roots to supplement the meagre supply of oxygen provided by its buried prop roots. Small fish shelter among the trees' roots, which offer protection from the larger predator fish, and at low tide, raccoon tracks can be seen where the animal searches for coon oysters firmly attached to the

SEEDS THAT TRAVEL THE SEAS

Even the seed pod is compatible with salt water, for the long green pod begins its development as a plant while aimlessly drifting with the currents, being transported until the warm waters place it in a strategic location for growth. At first, the seed floats horizontally — its body is buoyant in water — but as it is carried to and fro by the tides and currents, the roots begin to develop. The added cells increase the weight at one end, forcing the pod to float vertically until it is deposited on a suitable habitat for growth.

Once anchored to the bottom, the seed becomes very active, and, as all seeds do, it begins to anchor itself permanently by sending out roots. These roots absorb the nutrients from the soil, and a new plant is born, usually far from its parent plant. Less than half of all the thousands of seed pods grown annually remain in the vicinity of their origins; the remainder are swept out to sea with the changing tide, later moving at the will of the currents.

The new seedling sends out a tier of roots that arch out and finally downward to circle the new plant, offering support for new growth. Almost immediately the tangle of roots begins to accumulate dead plant material and pieces of broken shells cast about by tidal action. The young mangrove quickly captures material that will later help form a land mass where no land exists.

MANGROVE PLANT WITH SEEDLINGS

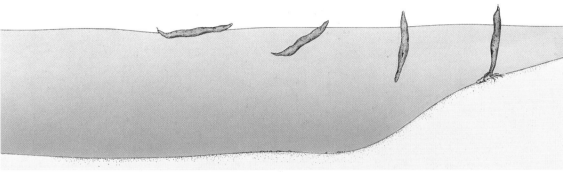

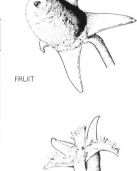

FRUIT

FLOWER

The red mangrove bears fruit and flowers simultaneously. The seedlings grow from the fruit while still on the parent tree and will drop into the water when they reach between 6 and 8 inches (15 and 20 cm) long.

root structure. Alligators also inhabit mangrove swamps, using it as a food source and as shade from the hot sun.

Mangroves provide much of the nutrition both directly and indirectly for life within the mangrove roots. The mangrove twigs and leaves decay and form humus, and this material is coated with bacteria, fungi and algae which aid decomposition. These tiny plants are eaten in turn by larger plants and form the beginning of the food chain in the swamp. This nursery for planktonic algae is of utmost importance to marine life, as algae is the basis of most marine chains.

Mangroves grow over much of the coastlines of Central and South America. Young shrimp find shelter among the roots, and the warmth of the water and the high nutritional value of the composted, decaying material encourages the growth of these shrimp so they mature into adults in a

decompose. Stormy waters bring rich food to the deeper waters as the storms recede, so that even the fringing reefs benefit from this valuable source of food.

Mangrove plants are surrounded by fine, soft, deep mud, formed as the tidal and river currents are slowed by the plants' roots. The sediment carried by those waters settles among the roots, a sediment rich in nutrients. In areas where mangroves flourish in a mixture of fresh water and salt water, the salt acts electrostatically on the finest particles of clay, causing them to sink among the roots which protect the particles from being stirred by wave action.

Mangroves the world over tend to grow in this fine mud rather than sand. The mud usually resembles quicksand, and when walking in the swamps it is necessary to cling to plants to avoid sinking deeply into the bottomless mire.

few months. As adults, they leave the safety of the mangroves at low tide, and move into the muddy estuaries where they are caught by the millions each year.

The swamps are havens for insects above the water and strange creatures below the surface. The waters are usually muddy, which is what makes this area of the shoreline so valuable. The soupy mass of silt and organic materials is so rich in nutrients and the temperatures so hot, that the marine life grows rapidly. Storms do not usually destroy the mangrove forest, but they do blow leaves and bark onto the water which then

ABOVE *Red mangrove plants have reclaimed the land; as the grass takes over, the red mangroves will die out.*

BELOW *This black mangrove tree has no support roots but does have breathing roots.*

The human threat

People have altered these tidal flats, however, by filling in many mangrove swamps for building purposes, little realizing what is really being destroyed. Worse yet is the building of embankments for roads crossing the middle of tidal flats. This cutting-in-half of the swamps leaves one side of the mangrove forest with a lack of salt-water balance and nutrients, thus stunting or killing entire forested areas.

LEFT *These shells and mangrove leaves make an attractive pattern on the ground. As the leaves decompose, they provide food; the shells will become tangled in the mangrove roots, mix with the mud and provide minerals for marine life.*

MANGROVE ISLANDS

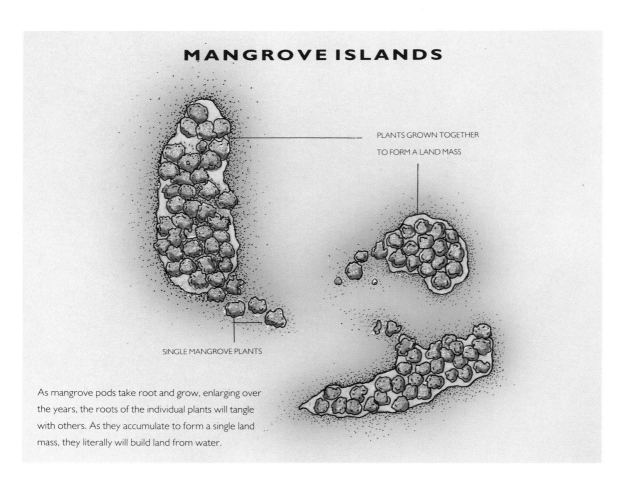

PLANTS GROWN TOGETHER
TO FORM A LAND MASS

SINGLE MANGROVE PLANTS

As mangrove pods take root and grow, enlarging over the years, the roots of the individual plants will tangle with others. As they accumulate to form a single land mass, they literally will build land from water.

In some parts of the Tropics, the red mangrove is an important source of tannin: the bark of this mangrove contains 20–30 per cent tannin in its raw state. When dried into a usable powder, the solid extract may contain up to 60 per cent tannin. Much of this is exported from the East Indies, East Africa and Central America and is used to tan leather.

Mature mangroves may reach heights of 100 ft (30 m) and have aerial roots 10 ft (3 m) high. The wood of this tree is hard, very heavy and much of it is cut into rafters and beams for use in buildings. As long as people do not take too much of the established forests for their own uses, the young mangroves will continue to reach farther and farther out into the shallow waters of the bay with the old, established trees building the shoreline. Some day the shallow bay will be land and someday the sea, in all its violence, will attack this new land and reclaim it, starting the process once again.

The canopy overhead plays just as important a role as the root system in the shore ecology. Large birds use the mature forest as roosting sites for protection from predatory animals. The larger wading birds and water fowl use these

ABOVE *An immature ibis standing in a mangrove tree. The trees provide a safe haven for birds.*

same protective trees to build nests and raise their young. Lying in the shadow of the younger mangroves on the forest fringe below are the smaller fish and reptiles that will provide the nourishment for the young birds in the nests.

The centre of a mangove forest may well have islands forming, small at first but enlarging as the years pass. As the mangroves accumulate enough material, two islands will join, making the land mass a little larger. Over hundreds of years the

mangrove plant, with its tangle of roots, will connect larger islands to one another. In fact, mangrove swamps are so effective in building land from water that the coastal swamps of Biscayne Bay and Florida Bay, on the southern end of Florida, US, have been responsible for adding 1,500 acres (607.5 ha) of new land over the last 40 years.

FIELD WORK IN THE MARSHES

THINGS
TO DO

▶ How many varieties of mangrove plants can you find and identify? Dip a plastic or glass container into the murky water and give the contents some time to settle before taking a look at how many visible life forms there are in it — look out for fishes.

GLOSSARY

ALGAE: a large group of plants which includes seaweed.

ANTENNAE: long, thin sensing devices which operate from the heads of invertebraes such as snails.

ARTHROPOD: an invertebrate animal with a segmented body and jointed legs, protected by a hard casing which is periodically shed.

BIVALVE: a type of mollusc whose body is enclosed by two shells.

CARNIVORE: a meat-eater.

CRUSTACEAN: a class of arthropods with external shells, including crabs, lobsters, shrimps and barnacles.

DETRITUS: pieces of debris from decaying plants and animals.

DIVER: some types of medium-large swimming bird.

EBB TIDE: the tide going out.

ECOLOGY: the study of the relationship between organisms and their surroundings.

EFFLUENT: waste waters, pumped into the sea and other waters by man.

ESTUARY: the area where a river mouth reaches the sea.

FILTER-FEEDER: an animal which feeds by filtering food from water (eg mussels).

FLOOD TIDE: the incoming tide.

FRONT: the leaves of seaweed.

GASTROPOD: a type of mollusc which moves about on a large, muscular foot.

GILLS: the organs through which fish, crustaceans and molluscs breathe.

HABITAT: the local area in which an organism lives.

HERBIVORE: an animal which feeds on vegetable matter.

INTERTIDAL: the area between the high and low tide marks.

INVERTEBRATE: an animal with no backbone.

LARVAE: immature animals which are very different from their adult forms.

MINERAL: naturally formed, inorganic substance with a particular chemical composition. For example salt is a mineral.

MOULT: to shed outer covering.

NORTH ATLANTIC DRIFT: the ocean current which flows north-eastwards across the north Atlantic towards northern Europe.

OMNIVORE: an animal which eats meat and vegetable matter.

PHOTOSYNTHESIS: the process through which green plants produce food molecules from carbon dioxide and water, using energy from the sun.

PLANKTON: tiny plants and animals which float in the sea.

PREDATOR: an animal which kills and feeds on living animals.

RECLAMATION: the recovery by man of land from the sea.

SALINITY: the degree of saltiness of the sea – this is usually measured in parts of salt per thousand parts of water.

SCAVENGER: an animal which feeds on debris such as dead bodies.

SHINGLE: grouping of small stones and pebbles, worn round and smooth by water.

SILT: fine-grained tiny particles of mineral matter.

SPLASH ZONE: the area o shore above the high water mark which is never covered by the tic but does receive sea spray.

STRANDLINE: the line of debris left on the high water mark.

SURF ZONE: the area where waves break.

TIDAL RANGE: the distance between the high and low water marks.

WADER: a kind of bird which lives in shallow-water habitats.

WRACK: one of the types of brown seaweed.

INDEX

Acknowledgements

Photographs were supplied by the following:

Frank S Balthis: pp20b, 35, 66c, 74b, 75b, 76, 77t.
Greenpeace Communications/Dorreboom: p21.
Alex Kerstitch: pp14t, 18, 19, 20t, 32tr, 37b, 38, 39b, 40tl, 43b, 44.
Don Kreuter: pp60, 61, 64, 65, 66bl, 67.
Bob Lollo: pp8, 10, 14b, 60br, 71, 72, 73.
Karen Lollo: pp7, 9, 11bl, 22, 23, 24, 25, 26, 27, 29, 30, 31tl, 31br, 32tl, 33tl, 33b, 34, 36, 37tr, 39t, 40br, 49, 50, 51, 52, 53, 54, 56, 57, 58bl, 58br, 60tr, 60bl, 68, 69, 70, 75t, 77b.
Scott Weidensaul: pp11tr, 12, 13, 15c, 15b, 16, 17, 28, 31r, 33tr, 40tr, 41b, 42, 43t, 43c, 45, 46, 47, 48, 58tl, 58tr, 59.

r = right, l = left, c = centre, t = top, b = bottom